Microsoft®

PowerPoint 2013®

Pocket Primer

Microsoft®

PowerPoint 2013®

Pocket Primer

Theodor Richardson

MERCURY LEARNING AND INFORMATION
Dulles, Virginia
Boston, Massachusetts
New Delhi

Publisher: David Pallai
MERCURY LEARNING AND INFORMATION
22841 Quicksilver Drive
Dulles, VA 20166
info@merclearning.com
www.merclearning.com
1-800-758-3756

T. Richardson. *Microsoft PowerPoint 2013 Pocket Primer.*
ISBN: 978-1-938549-90-8

The publisher recognizes and respects all marks used by companies, manufacturers, and developers as a means to distinguish their products. All brand names and product names mentioned in this book are trademarks or service marks of their respective companies. Any omission or misuse (of any kind) of service marks or trademarks, etc. is not an attempt to infringe on the property of others.

Library of Congress Control Number: 2013958095

1415321   Printed in the United States of America
This book is printed on acid-free paper.

Our titles are available for adoption, license, or bulk purchase by institutions, corporations, etc.

For additional information, please contact the Customer Service Dept. at 1-800-758-3756 (toll free). Digital versions of our titles are available at: *www.authorcloudware.com*

The sole obligation of MERCURY LEARNING AND INFORMATION to the purchaser is to replace the book and/or disc, based on defective materials or faulty workmanship, but not based on the operation or functionality of the product.

To my mother, Deborah Richardson; she is my calm voice of reason and one of the strongest people I have ever known. I am blessed to have you as my mother, and I love you very much.

CONTENTS

INTRODUCTION

I f you have ever wanted to learn about using Microsoft PowerPoint, along with productivity tools necessary for the modern business world, then this book is for you. You might be a new student who has little to no experience with this application or maybe you are a novice computer user wanting to learn to use presentation software; in either case, you should find this book to be a helpful and constructive companion on your journey.

This book covers the use of Microsoft PowerPoint 2013 for both Windows and Mac in a hands-on, project driven way that emphasizes both understanding and ability. You will practice using the software as you explore the different options it provides in a path of increasing complexity that, when mastered, will allow you to use this software day to day with confidence.

CHAPTER STRUCTURE

Each chapter is structured to provide an overview of the key concepts in order for you to demonstrate mastery at the completion of the chapter project. The sections on productivity software include a project for each chapter with detailed descriptions of how to use the various tools, functions, and commands in the respective software packages. In addition, we include the theory and history of how these applications have evolved and information on how these applications can be used to accomplish multiple tasks. Finally, "Knowledge Checks" are provided to test your comprehension of the chapters. Answers to these questions are provided at the back of the book.

Each chapter contains activities that give you hands-on practice as you move through the chapter. You will also be given practice exercises for basic comprehension and some challenge exercises to move you toward a higher level of mastery for the concepts presented in the chapter.

RESOURCE DVD

The textbook provides a DVD inside the back cover that includes resources for readers. This DVD includes 1) all of the files needed to complete the chapter exercises and activities within the text and 2) selected tutorial videos. You will also find a repository of high-resolution color images from the chapters and samples of completed projects for comparison.

ACKNOWLEDGMENTS

I am so pleased to have been involved with this book, and I want to thank David Pallai for taking the chance on publishing a book like this; his experience and guidance have shaped this into the book you hold in your hands. I also want to thank Katie Kennedy for her support, patience, and valuable assistance. I also want to thank my grandparents, Leonard and Sylvia Ullom, and my parents, Dan and Deborah Richardson, for giving me such a wonderful upbringing and helping me to capitalize on the opportunities that have led to my lifelong dream of seeing a book of my own creation in print. Thank you to everyone who worked on this project to meet the tight deadlines, and thank you to the readers who chose this book over others.

—Theodor Richardson

CHAPTER 1

REVIEW OF BASIC COMPUTING

In This Chapter

This chapter is a review of foundational computer concepts. If you have experience with basic computing and you would like to just learn the Office software, feel free to jump ahead to the next chapter. Otherwise, you will learn how to perform basic tasks on a computer in this chapter, including how to locate files and applications.

This chapter will teach you how to navigate and use the computer desktop environment. You will learn how to work in the computer environment using files and folders you develop from client applications available on your computer. You will also learn about navigating the environment by searching for files and folders as well as by using keyboard shortcuts to traverse the desktop environment. Once you have completed the chapter, you will be able to:

- Describe and identify elements of the user interface
- Navigate the desktop and locate applications, files, and folders
- Demonstrate the use of folders to organize files on your computer
- Construct and save files from basic applications

1.1 NAVIGATING THE DESKTOP

Whether you are using a Mac or a Windows-based computer while working your way through this text, navigation is done by interacting with the computer's *Graphical User Interface (GUI)*. The user interface is the visual (graphical) display provided by the computer's operating system that allows the user to visually interact and issue tasking commands into the BIOS. By interacting with the user interface, software applications can be started, closed, installed, and uninstalled.

The *Graphical User Interface* (or *GUI*) is the graphical display that allows the computer user to see the computer output and interact with the core components of the computer in a visual manner.

The *desktop* is the primary workspace for a graphical user interface; it is the digital equivalent of a physical desk. It typically contains menus to perform system functions and icons that represent applications or files on the computer system.

An *icon* is a small graphical representation of a program or command; clicking it usually starts a program or performs an action, depending on what the icon represents.

A *window* is an area of the screen acting as a standalone user interface to an application. A single application may use multiple windows (commonly one window per open file).

A *menu* is a selection of commands and options that are similar enough to form a group; the title of the menu is generally indicative of the type of commands it contains. Common examples of a menu are the File menu and Help menu.

A *toolbar* is a collection of icons that acts like the visual equivalent of a text menu, typically providing shortcuts to common commands and actions.

A *pane* is a section of a window with a specific purpose.

A *dialog box* is an encapsulated version of a user interface that is typically used for minor data entry or configuration. In most applications, an open dialog box has to be closed or otherwise dealt with to perform other tasks in the application.

1.2 INTRODUCTION TO THE WINDOWS OPERATING SYSTEM

The Microsoft Windows OS is a graphical interface used to interact with the computer and applications that reside on the hard disk. The new OS comes with many features that make working in the environment easy and convenient. Microsoft currently has two versions of its Windows Operating System that are still widely used in the market: Windows 7 and Windows 8. While most of the differences are cosmetic, the shift in Windows 8 is significant if you are familiar with previous versions of Windows. The next two sections will detail the basics of each of these versions.

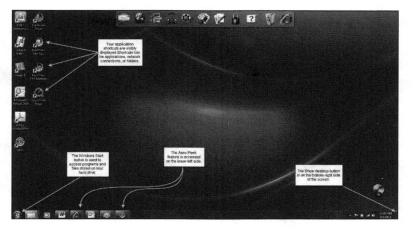

FIGURE 1.1 Windows 7 desktop

FIGURE 1.2 Using the Aero Peek feature

1.2.1 Windows 7

You can see the basic desktop environment in Figure 1.1. This is the view you will see after you login to your computer. You can see the layout is similar to previous versions of Windows, but there are some differences that increase the ease of use.

The taskbar at the bottom of the screen has a new *Aero Peek* feature that lets you view thumbnails (preview images) of running applications. You can place your mouse over the icon for the application to see a larger image as shown in Figure 1.2; this action displays a grouped image with a preview of all of the open windows for that application. By using the *Aero Peek* feature you can also close files from the thumbnails themselves by holding your mouse over the application group and selecting the *Close* icon (which looks like an *X*).

The *Show desktop* button on the bottom-right corner of the taskbar (shown in Figure 1.1) can be used to quickly alternate between the applications that are open by minimizing them with one click (of the left mouse button) and maximizing them with a second click.

By clicking on the Windows *Start* button in the lower-left corner you will see the menu shown in Figure 1.3. You have several options here, including

FIGURE 1.3 The Windows 7 Start menu

customizing the way listed applications appear. You can add programs to this initial menu list by right-clicking the mouse on the application you want to add and selecting *Add to start menu*. If you hold your mouse cursor (which looks like an arrow) over one of the applications, you will see all of the most recent files used within that particular application.

Another important task on an operating system is to identify the system information, including the software that is running on the machine and the hardware components of the system. In Windows 7, you can find the system information by selecting the *Start* menu, choosing Computer, and then selecting *System properties* in the window that opens. When you have followed this process, you will see a screen similar to the one shown in Figure 1.4.

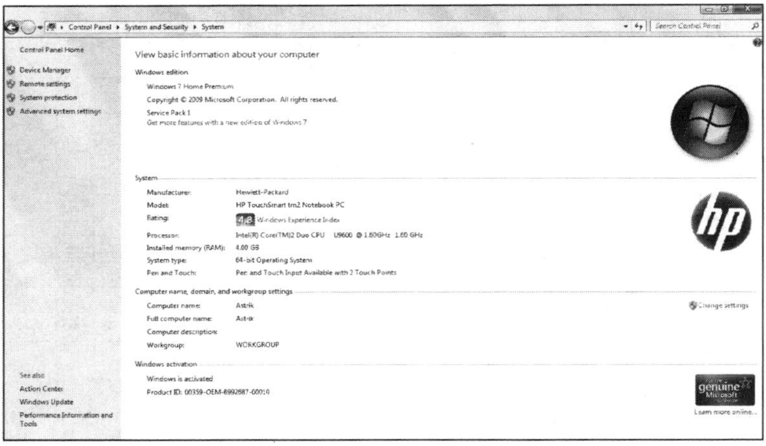

FIGURE 1.4 System properties for Windows 7

1.2.2 Windows 8

Instead of going straight to the desktop view, Windows 8 uses a Start screen which has icons for your installed applications and apps from the Windows store. The Desktop is one of the apps that is shown in the lower-right corner of the screen. You can click this icon to go the traditional Windows desktop view. You can see an example Start screen for Windows 8 in Figure 1.5.

The desktop environment for Windows 8 is very similar to Windows 7 in appearance. The Aero peek feature is included in Windows 8 as well as the

FIGURE 1.5 Windows 8 Start screen

full file and folder structure common to Windows 7, so you can create shortcut icons on the desktop and use Windows Explorer to view folder contents. You can see an example desktop for Windows 8 in Figure 1.6. To get back to the Start screen, you would simply click the *Windows logo* that appears in the lower-left corner of the interface. If you click and hold on the Windows logo, you will be prompted with a menu that includes the *Shut down or sign out* option to close down your computer from the software. You can also hold the power button to cycle through the shutdown procedure.

Because Windows 8 is made primarily for touch screen computers, most of the system activities you can perform are based on swiping left or right from the outside of the screen. Swiping in from the right to the center of the screen will open the menu for settings and customization. You can see an

FIGURE 1.6 Windows 8 desktop environment and swipe menu

example of this in Figure 1.6. To get the system information, you would swipe the right menu into view and choose *Settings* and then *PC info*. This will display the system information for the computer.

1.2.3 The Windows Desktop

In the previous section, you were introduced to the Windows desktop environment, which is the computer's user interface. One of the primary functions

FIGURE 1.7 Windows 7 Start button

of a user interface is to help humans visually interact with the computer and utilize the software programs available for various activities. Accessing the software programs on your computer can be done in one of two ways: by using the *Start* button in Windows 7 (or the *Start screen* in Windows 8) shown in Figure 1.7 or by *double-clicking* on a particular shortcut icon on the desktop (double-clicking is two rapid clicks using the left button on your mouse) or in the folder in which the application is installed.

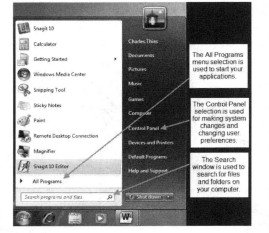

FIGURE 1.8 Windows 7 Start menu

The *mouse* is the hardware device you use to move the cursor on the computer screen over the desktop to interact with programs and files. You can begin your exploration by moving your cursor (by moving the mouse) to the *Start* button and pressing the left button on the mouse one time. Performing this action will activate the Start menu, shown in Figure 1.8.

1.2.3.1 The Control Panel

The right side of the Start menu in Windows 7 has several fixed options, one of which is the Control Panel option. The Control Panel (shown in Figure 1.9) gives the user the ability to make system setting changes. This includes hardware and software installations and uninstallations (uninstalls). The Control Panel in Windows 8 is accessed by swiping in the right side, choosing *Settings* and then selecting *Control Panel*. This will activate a window similar to the Windows 7 Control Panel.

Notice the Appearance and Personalization submenu in the Control Panel. Selecting this option brings up several options available to customize your desktop environment, as shown in Figure 1.10.

Notice in the *Appearance and Personalization* submenu in Figure 1.10 that you can personalize your desktop by changing the desktop theme, colors, and background. This submenu is also where you will find the display properties

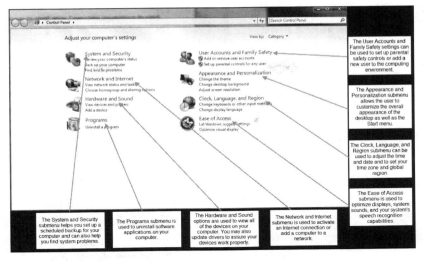

FIGURE 1.9 Windows 7 Control Panel

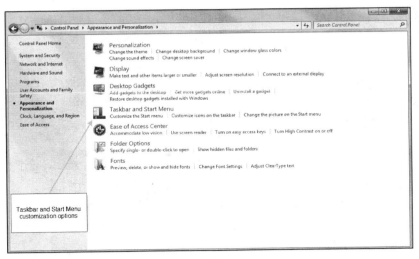

FIGURE 1.10 Appearance and Personalization options

where you can adjust your graphics card's properties such as its screen resolution and whether you use one screen or two screens.

1.2.3.2 Jump Lists

Another feature to help you navigate the desktop more efficiently is a Jump List. *Jump Lists* allow a user to quickly open a recent file from an application on the taskbar or a pinned application on the Start menu, as shown in Figure 1.13. You can also pin items to Jump Lists on the taskbar, which is available in Windows 8 as well.

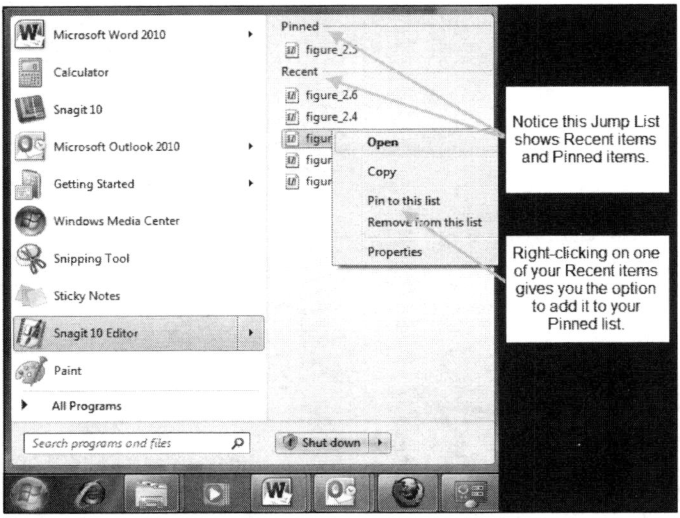

FIGURE 1.11 Jump List

1.2.3.3 Task Manager

Sometimes a program on your computer may lock up and cease to function. Most of the time Windows will automatically send you a warning and either restart the program or close it completely. If for some reason the program does not close, you can open the *Task Manager* and end a process that has stopped working by pressing the *End Task* button at the bottom of the window shown in Figure 1.12.

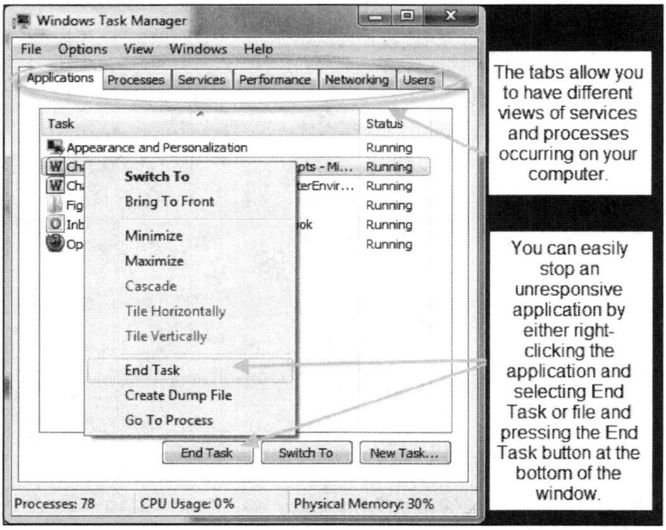

FIGURE 1.12 Task Manager

You can open the Task Manager in two ways. First, you can simply move the pointer to the taskbar, right-click, and select *Task Manager* from the menu that appears. The second way to get to the Task Manager is to use the keyboard shortcut by pressing *Ctrl+Shift+Esc*. The Task Manager displays programs and services that are running on your computer at the time you open the window. You can also use the Task Manager to view network processes or users logged into your system. In Windows 8, a shortened Task Manager appears when it is first activated. You can view the full details by choosing the *More details* option.

A *keyboard shortcut* is a particular combination of keys pressed at the same time and is used to access menus or other services efficiently without the use of the mouse.

1.2.3.4 Libraries Feature

Over time you may accumulate a large number of files and folders on your desktop, which can make navigating the desktop difficult. Libraries are a feature in Windows that can help you find and organize your files in one consolidated location. This allows you to save time by having one place where all of your files and folders can easily be located. To access the Libraries feature, click the *Libraries* icon on the lower-left side of the taskbar. A visual reference of the Libraries icon can be seen in Figure 1.13. The Libraries window has a search box that allows the user to search for files and folders using options such as Kind, Date modified, Type, and Name as search criteria.

You can see by looking at Figure 1.13 that there are four standard libraries: Documents, Music, Pictures, and Videos. You can also create new libraries to help you organize your collections of files and folders. To create a new library, highlight the *Libraries* selection at the left side of the window, as shown in Figure 1.13, and right-click. This will produce a new menu; select *New,* then

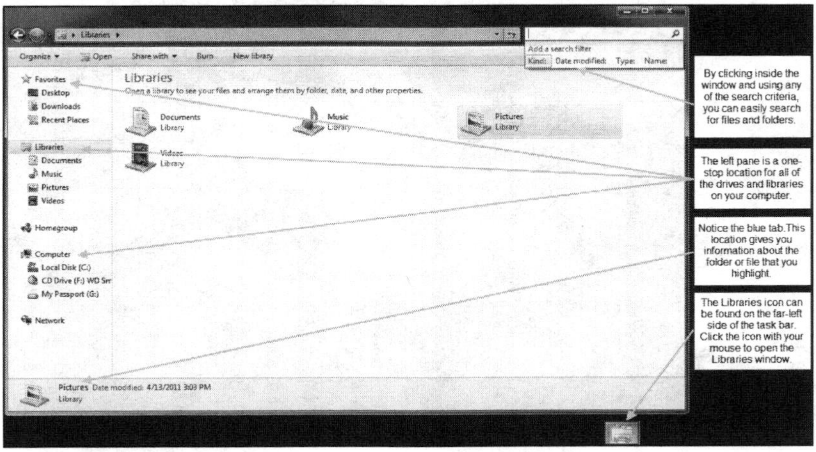

FIGURE 1.13 Libraries window

Library and name the new library folder. For example, this might be a library for all of your schoolwork. You might name the library *Undergraduate* or give it the name of the school you are attending and then have subfolders in the library for each course that you are taking.

1.3 INTRODUCTION TO MAC OS X

This section is an introduction to the elements of the Macintosh OS X desktop. The Mac OS X platform is a graphical interface used to interact with the computer and applications that reside on the hard disk and works in a manner similar to the Windows platform. When you first log into your computer, you are in the *Finder* window as displayed in Figure 1.14; this is the equivalent of a PC desktop or workspace.

The Mac platform is credited with being one of the most user-friendly operating systems, as well as an operating system that faces far fewer security threats than the Windows platform. If you are new to the Apple platform and are used to Microsoft's products, there is a significant learning curve involved.

Menu extras are located on the top right-hand portion of the Mac OS window and let you control system volume or manage your Internet connections as illustrated in Figure 1.14.

The Mac platform can perform the same tasks that a Windows machine can, although sometimes different procedures are necessary to achieve equivalent functionality. The iMac desktop shown in Figure 1.14 contains display

FIGURE 1.14 The Mac OS X Finder window

features you might not recognize, but you must learn about these as a first step toward building proficiency with the Mac OS X platform.

Along the right side of the screen you will find the *Macintosh HD* icon. It is important to note that Apple prefers users to keep their desktops clear of any icons. If you are using the Mountain Lion or newer version, you should not have anything on the desktop at all unless you upgraded from a previous version and you kept those icons on your desktop.

The *Dock* is the launcher for all of your programs and files; it is located along the bottom of the interface. The *Dock* has a *divider* line designed to keep applications on the left side and files and folders on the right side. You can easily drag new programs to the Dock or remove them by dragging them off of the Dock. The *Apple* menu, shown earlier in the chapter, is used to shut down the computer or put it in sleep mode. You are also able to initiate software updates and adjust system preferences here.

The *Sidebar* (shown in Figure 1.15) is located on the left-side pane of every Finder window. The sidebar has four sections: Devices, Shared, Places, and Search For. A double left-click (hereafter referred to simply as a double-click) on an application's icon opens that application. Minimizing applications is a matter of clicking on the yellow button at the top left of any application window; the application minimizes to the right side of the Dock. Chapter 2 will continue the exploration and use of the Macintosh OS X interface. As of OS X Mavericks, tabs are allowed in the Finder windows as well.

The Apple menu (as shown in Figure 1.14 on the upper-left corner of the interface) is where you can shut down or restart your system. Choosing the

FIGURE 1.15 The Mac OS X sidebar in the Finder window

About This Mac selection provides information about system specifics such as operating system version and basic capability. Choosing *Restart* gives you the ability to restart your system, which is often necessary after system updates or software installation. It is important to save all of your important files prior to restarting your system to avoid losing important information.

ACTIVITY 1.1—SYSTEM INFORMATION

For this activity, you will follow the process for getting the system information from your computer. This should include the version of the OS that is in use along with the profile of hardware included on your machine. Follow the instructions provided for your OS in the previous sections and describe the information that is presented. When would this be useful or necessary information to have?

1.3.1 The Macintosh OS X Desktop

Although the Mac has a similar appearance, it is different from a Windows-based PC. Unlike the Windows platform, many of the desktop settings on the Mac can be found in the *Apple* menu. As you might remember from previous sections, the *Apple* menu is accessed by clicking the Apple icon (shown in Figure 1.16) at the top-left side of the menu bar.

FIGURE 1.16 Apple icon to access the Apple menu

Starting an application also works much differently than on a Windows machine. In a Windows environment, you may have used the Start screen or Start button to access all of your settings and applications. On a Mac, all of the applications you use regularly reside on the *Dock* near the bottom of the interface (as shown in Figure 1.17).

FIGURE 1.17 The Dock

To access applications on a Mac, you can start them either from the Dock or from the application's icon in the *Applications* folder. It is easy to add or remove applications from the Dock. You can simply click on a program icon and drag it away from the Dock to remove the application. To add an application to the Dock, you simply click on the application you want in the Applications folder and drag it to the left side of the divider (the dotted white vertical line) on the Dock. You can click and drag icons on the Dock to reorder them.

The *Dock* is the collection of program icons at the bottom of the Mac desktop screen used to quickly access the applications you use most frequently.

1.3.1.1 The Finder

If you are using a new implementation of the Mac OS X system, there is nothing on your desktop and you might be wondering how you access applications because there is so much more available than what you see on the Dock. The applications on your computer are found in the *Applications* folder. You can use the Finder window to access the Applications folder by clicking on the *Finder* program icon on the Dock (see Figure 1.18).

FIGURE 1.18
Finder program icon

If you do not have any applications running, you will notice that the Finder menu is available at the top of your screen. You can alternatively click on the background of the screen and the active application menu will be the Finder application. If a Finder window does not appear, you can select the *Go* option on the *Finder* menu, as shown in Figure 1.19.

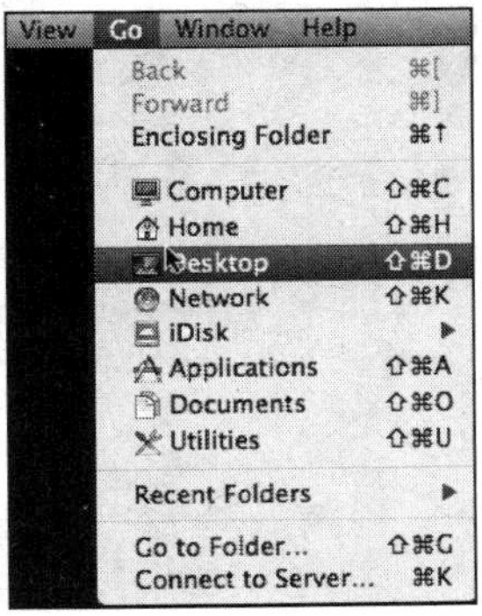

The Go menu gives you the ability to navigate to different areas on your computer system. You will notice that to the right of the options are your shortcut keys. Mac has a wide selection of shortcut keys you can use to quickly navigate to areas within your system and perform common tasks.

FIGURE 1.19 The Finder menu Go selection

1.3.1.2 The Dock

If the Dock is too small or too large for your personal preference, you can quickly and easily adjust its size by selecting the *Apple* menu, then the *Dock* selection, and finally *Dock Preferences* to open the window shown in Figure 1.20. Now you can simply move the Size slider to increase or decrease the size of the Dock.

One final feature on the Dock that you may need is the ability to view hidden menus. If you are simply taking a look at your program icons, it is not

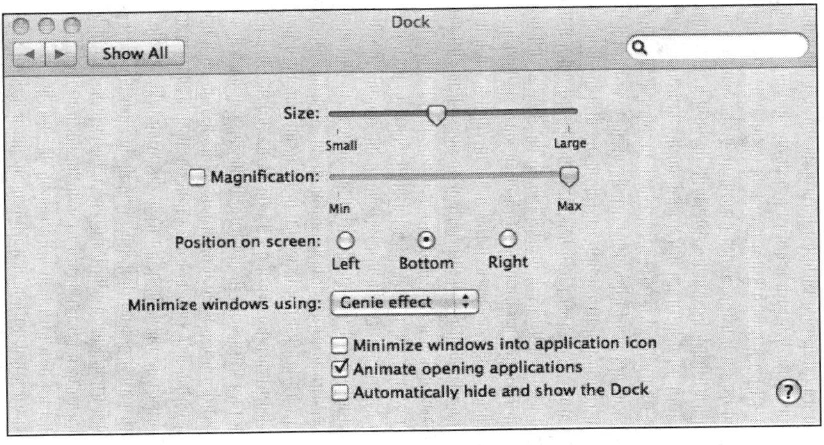

FIGURE 1.20 Dock Preferences window

FIGURE 1.21 Hidden menu for the Mail application

immediately apparent that there are more options available to the user. Simultaneously pressing the *Ctrl* button and clicking on a particular program's icon (the Mail icon in Figure 1.21) displays the hidden menu for that program.

You can clearly see there are additional options in the hidden menu. At the top of the menu in Figure 1.21, you can see that there is an open associated file. Clicking on the open file labeled *TOC* brings up an email window. You can perform this action with any of your applications on the Dock or the OS X desktop to view hidden menus.

1.3.1.3 The Dashboard, Exposé, and Spaces

In the OS X environment, you have widgets available in the *Dashboard*. When you activate the Dashboard (which will then appear to float over your desktop), you will see that it contains a clock, calendar, calculator, and the weather. You can use the Dashboard's hidden menu to change your Dashboard settings or add new widgets you find online. You can also change your Dashboard settings by accessing the *Apple* menu and selecting *System Preferences*. System Preferences is also where you can adjust settings for Exposé and Spaces.

Exposé and Spaces are features within the Mac OS X environment that make desktop navigation and organization a breeze. Exposé is similar to the Aero Peek feature in Windows 7; both of these give you a preview of the applications you have open and let you open one by moving your cursor to it and clicking. With most keyboards, you simply press the *F3* key to view the Exposé of active applications.

Rather than placing a preview at the bottom of the taskbar for minimized applications, Exposé places your open and minimized application windows in small preview windows laid out so that you can see every application you have open at once as shown in Figure 1.23. Clicking on one of the application windows maximizes the window and brings you to the desired application.

FIGURE 1.22 Dashboard displaying widgets on desktop and hidden menu snippet

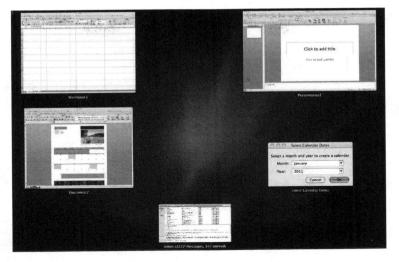

FIGURE 1.23 Active Exposé view

Spaces is the other tab on the Exposé & Spaces configuration window. The Spaces feature lets you organize the applications on your desktop in a way that is efficient to the way you work. This feature allows you to assign applications to one of four spaces on your desktop. In Figure 1.24, you can see that if you select the + symbol you can add desired applications to a particular quadrant. This way, each time you open an application on the Dock, it appears in the quadrant you have selected.

FIGURE 1.24 Spaces configuration settings

1.3.1.4 Force Quit

If you want to stop an unresponsive application when using the Macintosh OS, you must use the *Force Quit* option. It is important that you only use the Force Quit option if you are absolutely unable to work with the application and it is unresponsive. Using this option will cause the application to close without saving any work. You can Force Quit out of an application by selecting the *Force Quit* option from the *Apple* menu. As an alternative, you can press the *Command+Option+Esc* keys simultaneously. You must then select the unresponsive application from the menu that appears.

ACTIVITY 1.2—PROCESS MONITORING

Use either the Task Manager in Windows or the Activity Monitor in Mac OS X (located in the Applications/Utilities folder under the hard drive). Identify the processes and applications that are running on your machine. Describe the information about each process or application that is being presented to you. How is this information useful for managing the computer system?

1.4 ORGANIZING FILES AND FOLDERS

Organizing files and folders is an essential task on a computer. By organizing your files effectively, you can quickly find documents you need. Part of this organization process is the use of folders to group similar content. These work just like real folders that you can use to organize paper documents. The fundamental principles are the same, regardless of the operating system you use. Each folder can contain subfolders in a hierarchical arrangement. Ultimately, all of your folders will stem from one source, such as your hard drive (typically labeled C on a Windows machine); the folders within that are subfolders, and each of those can contain subfolders. Even your desktop is a subfolder of the hard drive on which your operating system is stored.

1.4.1 Files and Folders in Windows

Organizing files and folders on Windows is a common task, and there are many features that can be quite helpful if used properly. One of the first things to start off with is storing files in appropriate folders. Think of organizing files and folders on your computer as similar to organizing a filing cabinet at your home or office. Assume you wanted to use your filing cabinet to store all of your homework assignments for your first semester of undergraduate education. If you are taking four courses, you might make four folders. For this example, pretend you are taking Biology, Math, Sociology, and Business Ethics.

Creating your folders with categories is the first step to help you sort all of the documents you will quickly begin to accumulate during the semester. If your courses are eight weeks long, you might want eight subfolders to store assignments by week. This might require that you now create 8 subfolders for each course category for a total of 32 subfolders. Once you have your filing cabinet categorized with folders and subfolders, you can begin to populate them with assignments, tests, and quizzes for each week of the semester. Each one of these documents you collect is part of the set of files that will populate your filing cabinet.

To translate this to the environment of the computer, the filing cabinet on the computer is located in the chosen storage location on the media you select. Recall from the previous chapter that media can be the computer's internal hard drive, an external hard drive, or a thumb drive that you use to store all of your important data. In the following example, you will use the *My Documents* folder (accessible via the Libraries functionality) to create a file structure to store your school documents.

NOTE

You can create a folder anywhere on your hard drive, external media, or desktop. Windows contains a default folder you can use for this purpose called My Documents. *The problem, though, is that if you just drop all of your documents in there, over time it can become a mess. Imagine having to scroll through 75 files. It is not as hard as you might think to accumulate that many files in a short amount of time. A great place to start the project of organizing your documents is to create your folders in the My Documents folder for each category of organization you want to have, such as folders for Home, Work, and School.*

You can see in Figure 1.25 that the Libraries and Documents selections on the left have been expanded and the My Documents folder is highlighted. The My Documents folder shown here does not have any files in it. Highlighting the My Documents folder opens the folder for you to view its contents. In this case, the folder simply has a title at the top of the window indicating the

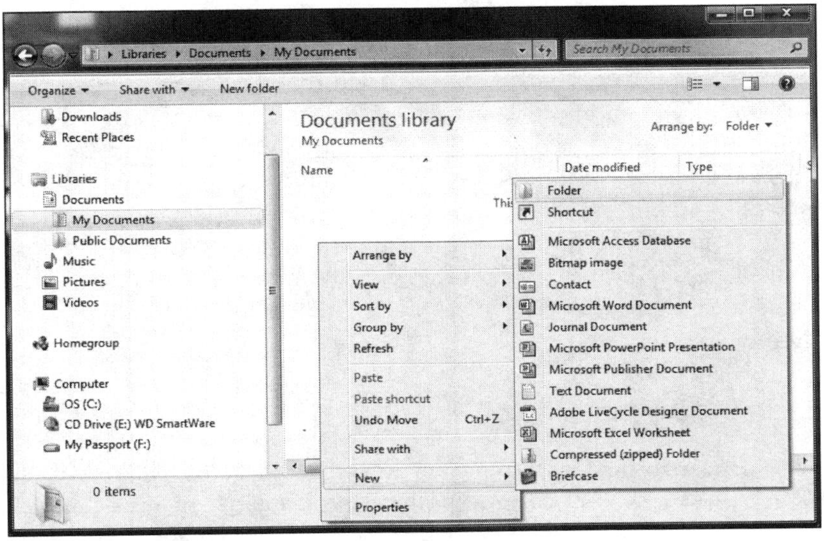

FIGURE 1.25 Using the Windows Libraries feature to create a new folder

Documents library in green letters and *My Documents* in black letters. Now simply right-click with your mouse pointer in the window and a menu appears with New as an option near the bottom. Selecting *New* gives you many options, as shown in the menu at the right; one of them is the creation of a new folder.

Selecting *Folder* creates a new folder as shown in Figure 1.26 with the title *New folder* highlighted in blue. This indicates you can proceed to type a desired name for the new folder. You should always take care to title your folders immediately, or you may forget what they contain or what their original purpose was supposed to be.

Documents library	Arrange by: Folder ▼	
My Documents		
Name	Date modified	Type
New folder	4/18/2011 9:25 PM	File folder

FIGURE 1.26 A new folder in the My Documents folder

Documents library	Arrange by: Folder ▼	
My Documents		
Name	Date modified	Type
School	4/18/2011 9:25 PM	File folder

FIGURE 1.27 The new School folder in the My Documents folder

Now take a look at Figure 1.27 where the newly created *School* folder resides in the My Documents location of your computer; you can think of this as your School category. Now you can add subfolders that reside within this School folder. For example, you might create a subfolder within the School folder titled Biology, indicating a storage location for all of the work you complete and collect for the science course you are taking, and you can create a subfolder within that for each week during the term.

In Figure 1.28, you can see there are now four subfolders within the main School folder. Each subfolder represents a course you are taking. You could further develop each subfolder by adding subfolders representing each week in your school term.

ACTIVITY 1.3—CREATING A FOLDER

Create a new folder on your computer named *Activity2_2*. Move the folder to the proper location on your machine for saving documents. Describe the process of creating the folder and the process of navigating to the proper location for documents to reside on the computer.

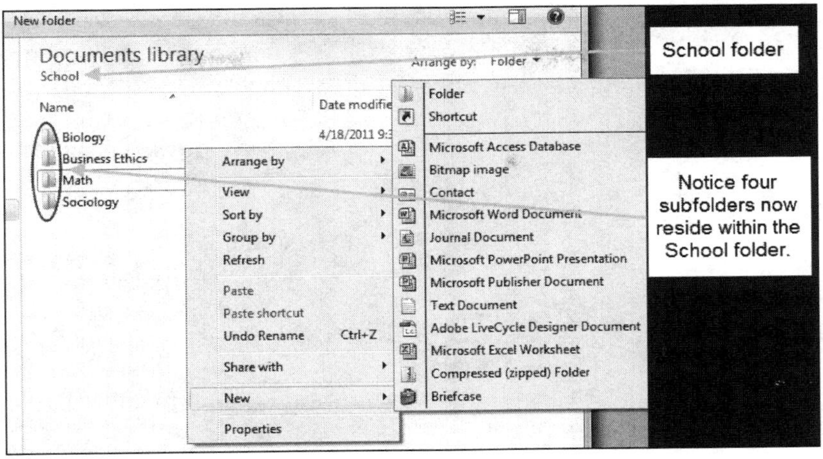

FIGURE 1.28 School folder with new subfolders

1.4.2 Files and Folders on a Mac

Organizing files and folders on a Mac is essential. If you have read the previous sections relating to the Mac environment, then you have already been introduced to the place where you will start. Your starting point is the Finder window, where you can access all of the applications and folders on your computer. You can actually create folders anywhere on the Mac including the desktop, but the current Mac culture encourages users to keep the desktop clean. For this example, you will begin by creating a filing system for your school documents in the *Documents* folder, as shown in Figure 1.29.

To create the main folder titled *School*, double-click on the *Documents* folder to open it. The Documents folder in this instance contains only a Microsoft User Data folder that stores the preference settings for the Microsoft Office 2011 suite of applications. (The Snagit folder stores images for a screen capture application.) The School folder will be used to file schoolwork. Notice in Figure 1.29 how the button with a gear and a drop-down arrow is activated. A new menu has appeared beneath it. Select *New Folder* to create a folder.

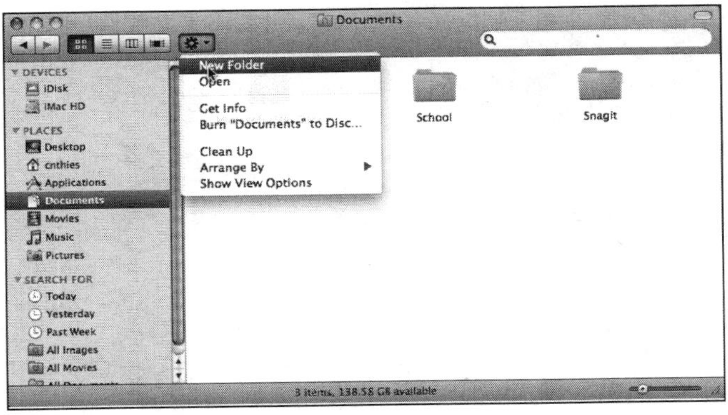

Once the new folder appears on the desktop, you have the option to name the folder. In this case, name it *School*. Now if

FIGURE 1.29 Finder window

FIGURE 1.30 School folder in Finder window

you were to dump all of your assignments in the School folder without any further organization, the folder would quickly become very cluttered and disorganized. The next step is to create subfolders for each subject that will reside in the School folder. Open the *School* folder and create four subfolders, as shown in Figure 1.30. Subfolders are created in the same way you created the School folder.

The *subfolder* is simply a folder that resides within another folder.

FIGURE 1.31 Subfolders broken down into weeks

Because you do not want clutter in your subfolders, you can create additional subfolders within your course subject for the weeks of the course as shown in Figure 1.31. You can name these new subfolders by week so that you can categorize and store each week's assignments in an organized fashion. Once you have finished creating this new structure, you will notice that this filing method matches a hierarchical structure. Following a similar format for data storage of all types will help you stay organized as you work with your computer.

1.5 WORKING WITH FILES ON YOUR COMPUTER

Now that you have learned about getting around on your system and developing a filing structure to organize application files, you can begin learning about files. A *file* can be an application document or image that can be stored on digital media, either externally or internally (such as on your computer hard drive). You have already learned about applications on your computer system, so it is time to put them to use.

You are probably reading this text to learn to use productivity software to construct professional presentations, databases, and other professional documents. Before you approach that task, you should get started with one of the basic applications that came with your personal computer to introduce you to the concept of a file. There are a couple of things you need to know about files. You may recall an earlier discussion on the concept of storage space on your computer in both the forms of available space on your hard drive and other media devices you use to store files. Before saving a file, you need to know where you will save it and the type of file it will be saved as. All files are associated with a file extension, which is usually a period (or decimal point) followed by three letters. For example, the name *mytext.txt* is a valid filename. You get to define the part to the left of the period, but the part to the right should come from a list of existing file types so your machine can recognize it and know how to process the information.

1.5.1 WordPad on Windows

WordPad is a basic word-processing application on the Windows platform. To start WordPad in Windows 7, click with your pointer on the *Start* menu and select *All Programs* and then the *Accessories* folder. Within the *Accessories* folder, you will find the WordPad icon. Click on the *WordPad* icon to start the application. In Windows 8, you can access WordPad by swiping in the menu on the right, selecting Search, and typing "WordPad" in the search box.

Enter the following message in the WordPad interface: *This is my first WordPad document. I am going to save it for future reference.* (See Figure 1.32.) If you are following along with your own version of WordPad, then congratulations, you have just created your first WordPad document.

We will not go into a lot of the functionality of WordPad here because you will be learning about more advanced Office applications in the next several chapters; just keep in mind that there is a lot you can do with it. If you have no other alternative, you can use WordPad to type documents and then open them later in the Microsoft Word application by using a file extension that Word understands.

Every application file needs to be saved with a file extension. Every application opens files based on the file extension with which it was saved. Now that you have created your first WordPad document, you must save it to avoid losing the information. Saving the document will allow you to reopen it at a future date.

To save your new WordPad file, select the *WordPad* button shown at the top left of Figure 1.33, and then select *Save as* and *Rich Text document*.

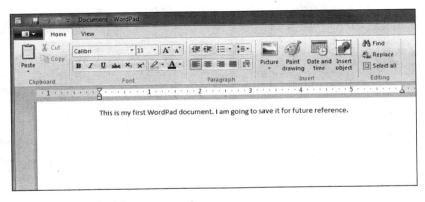

FIGURE 1.32 WordPad document sample

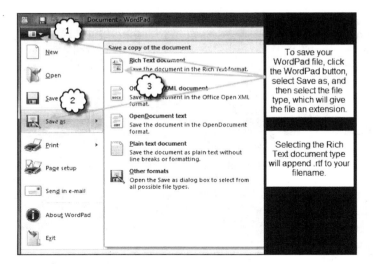

FIGURE 1.33 Saving a WordPad file

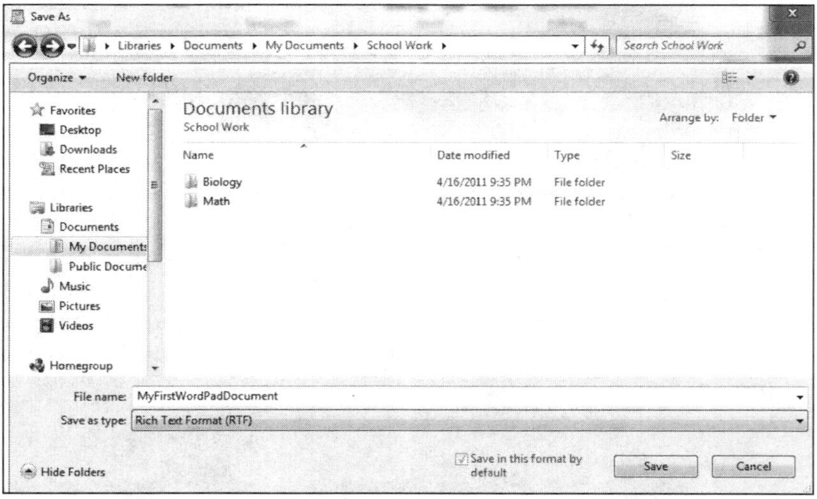

FIGURE 1.34 Using the Libraries feature to select the location for your new file

The file extension associates your new file with the applications that can open your file. It is important to keep in mind that sometimes more than one application may have the capability to open your file but may not be set as the primary application. In such cases, you should open the application you wish to use and open the file manually from within that application.

Now that you have selected to save your new WordPad file as a Rich Text Format (RTF) file, the Libraries menu comes up on your desktop. You may remember that earlier you created the folder structure for your school folders, which you developed inside your My Documents folder.

In the *Libraries* dialog that appears on the desktop, as shown in Figure 1.36, expand the *Documents* library and open the *School* folder you created. Once you have the location selected, place your cursor in the *File name* text box and type the name for your new file, which in this case is *MyFirstWordPadDocument*. Be sure the correct file type extension, *Rich Text Format (RTF)* in this case, is selected in the *Save as type* text box. Finally, press the *Save* button to save your new WordPad file to your chosen location. To view the properties of the file, select the file location, right-click on the icon for the file, and select Properties. This will open a new window with the file properties, such as size, date created, date modified, and the program that is assigned to open the file.

1.5.2 TextEdit for Macintosh

It is important to note that with any operating system you will use file extensions. Every time you save a new file, you have the opportunity to select the file type, which gives the file a new extension to associate it with an application that is able to open it. On the Macintosh, you have an application similar to WordPad called TextEdit. The TextEdit application also enables you to develop documents and even save the file as a Microsoft Word document. Notice in Figure 1.35 that the File Format options include some of the older Microsoft Word formats.

The TextEdit application can be found in the Applications folder on your Macintosh computer and can be located using the Finder application in the Dock on your desktop. Once you have the application open, type the following in the main document pane: *This is my first TextEdit document. I am going to save it for future reference.*

Locate the Documents folder in the Finder view, as shown in Figure 1.36, and save the file to the *School* folder you created earlier when you developed a file structure for all of your schoolwork. Notice the

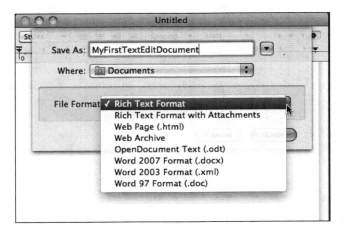

FIGURE 1.35 Choosing the file type for a sample TextEdit document

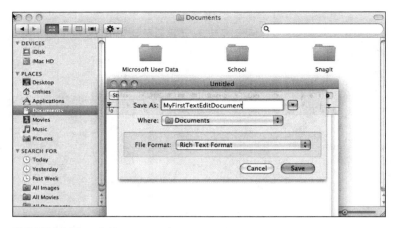

FIGURE 1.36 Sample Documents view

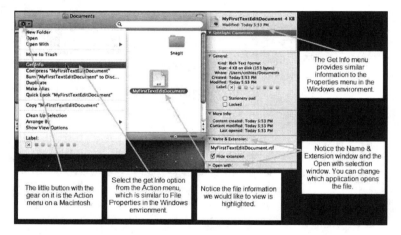

FIGURE 1.37 Viewing file information on the Macintosh

Untitled Save as window gives you the option to save the file with a name that you choose, which in this case is *MyFirstTextEditDocument*.

After selecting where to save the file (the *Documents* folder) and the file format (*Rich Text Format*), it's time to save the file by pressing the *Save* button. To examine the properties of the file you created in TextEdit, simply return to the folder where you stored it in the *Documents* folder, as shown in Figure 1.37.

Click on the file named *MyFirstTextEditDocument* and click on the Action menu. From the Action menu, you can select *GetInfo*; the menu appears very similar to what you would see in the Windows environment showing the file properties. From this menu, you can change the file extension type and even the program that opens the file.

ACTIVITY 1.4—FILE PROPERTIES

Using the file you created in the text editor, follow the process to examine the file properties for your OS. Explain the information that is presented and the options you have to change the file or its behavior. When would this be useful in managing documents?

CHAPTER SUMMARY

This chapter provided an introduction to navigating the Windows and Macintosh desktops in an efficient manner. It covered the user interface on both operating systems and gave users an introduction to modifying system preferences and managing documents. Managing files and folders are an important part of using any computer system. You should now be able to create folders and subfolders to effectively organize your personal computing filing system. The next chapter focuses on the paradigm of cloud computing, particularly the OneDrive which integrates directly with Microsoft Office.

CHAPTER KNOWLEDGE CHECK

1. The _____ is the graphical display provided by the computer's operating system that allows the user to visually interact with and issue tasking commands to the Basic Input/Output System.
   a. User interface
   b. iPad2
   c. Visual display
   d. Both a and b

2. To remove a program from the Start menu, simply right-click and then click _____ from the Start menu.
   a. Delete
   b. Unpin
   c. Rename
   d. None of the above

3. The Windows desktop is almost identical in Windows 7 and Windows 8, with the Start menu and Start screen being the primary difference.
   a. True
   b. False

4. It is possible to change the desktop appearance on both a Windows PC and a Mac.
   a. True
   b. False

5. The Apple menu and the Start menu contain all of the same options.
   a. True
   b. False

PRACTICE EXERCISES

1. Think about a category of files you would like to organize on your computer's hard drive or an external media device. It could be any set of files on your computer, such as digital images or documents. Plan and develop a filing system to help you organize these files. Write a short document that describes the folder and subfolder setup you would develop to organize files stored on your computer system. You can complete this assignment in either the Macintosh or Windows environment.

2. Use the Appearance and Personalization selection within the Control Panel to change your Windows desktop theme. If you are using the Mac, use the System Preferences to modify your desktop. Briefly explain the process you used.

3. Conduct basic research on the different types of file extensions. Make a list of at least five different types of file extensions. Each file extension associates a stored file with a certain application. Construct a table that displays the types of file extensions you listed and their compatible applications.

4. Construct a Venn diagram that compares and contrasts the Macintosh and Windows interfaces. Next, write a brief paragraph explaining which interface you prefer for your daily use and why.

2

MICROSOFT ONEDRIVE AND CLOUD COMPUTING

With the increasing power of the Internet and the decrease in cost of server space, a new paradigm for data storage has arisen in cloud computing. Cloud computing is a means to remotely store or process data on a server so you can access it anywhere you have a connection to the Internet. Microsoft's cloud service, OneDrive, allows you to store your files remotely from your desktop or from any of the common Microsoft Office applications. This chapter covers the basics of creating an account in the cloud and using it to enhance your own productivity. Once you complete this chapter, you will be able to:

- Create an account with Microsoft OneDrive
- Store and retrieve files from your cloud storage location
- Connect your desktop to your cloud storage
- Integrate your OneDrive account with Microsoft Office

2.1 CLOUD COMPUTING

Cloud computing is the use of remote resources to process information or store files. The benefit of cloud storage is the ability to connect to these files and folders wherever you are as long as you have a connection to the Internet. This frees you from using one machine or carrying the files on physical storage media from place to place. This can also be a beneficial backup for meetings or presentations where you may need to access a secondary copy of a file if the storage media fails or you do not have your original computer with you. As Internet connectivity becomes more advanced and storage space on servers becomes cheaper, cloud computing and cloud storage have become much more popular options for file management.

Even though cloud computing is convenient, there is a security risk with storing your files outside of your computer. You should keep this in mind with the type of information and documents you place in your cloud storage system. Do not store anything containing personal information like your social security number or bank account information in the cloud; it is too easy for it to become compromised or to be intercepted over the network as you store or retrieve it.

2.2 MICROSOFT ONEDRIVE

Microsoft OneDrive is a free cloud storage service from Microsoft. It integrates with both the Windows and Macintosh desktop systems and allows for access on remote devices like smart phones and tablets. The free version of OneDrive comes with 7 GB of storage, but you can pay to upgrade this if you have higher needs than this. OneDrive also allows access to the Web app versions of Word, PowerPoint, and Excel.

NOTE *If you have setup a Microsoft Windows Live Hotmail address, the login and password you use for that will serve as your account on OneDrive as well.*

2.2.1 Creating a Microsoft Account

OneDrive can be accessed from the Web at *www.onedrive.com*; this will reroute you to a custom URL where you can login or create an account. The interface for the OneDrive homepage is shown in Figure 2.1. If you have a Microsoft account, you can login with it at this page to access the OneDrive without creating a new account.

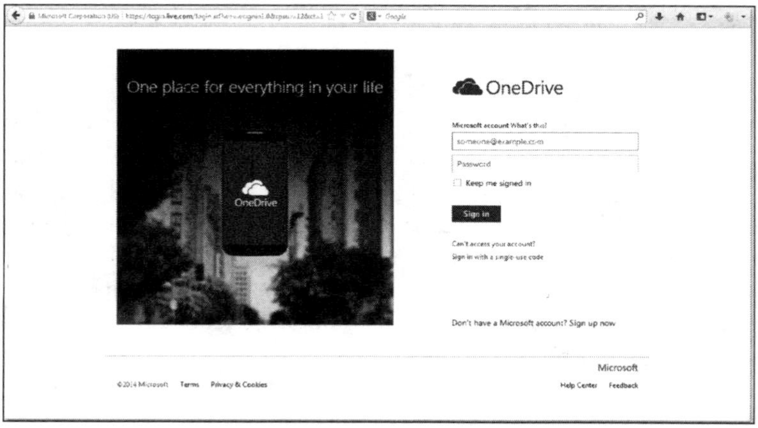

FIGURE 2.1 OneDrive homepage

If you do not have a Microsoft account, you can create one for using the OneDrive by clicking the Sign up now link at the bottom of the screen. When you click this link, it will redirect you to the page where you can setup a Microsoft account.

From SkyDrive to OneDrive

NOTE *Microsoft's cloud computing platform was previously called SkyDrive. This is the same service that is now called OneDrive; it has simply been rebranded. You may encounter the term SkyDrive on platforms that have not been fully updated, but rest assured you are accessing the same system with all of your saved files.*

This process is similar to creating a Microsoft Windows Live Hotmail account, in which you must create a username, password, and enter some identifying details like your address and an additional form of contact that can be used to verify the account. Once you have completed this process, you can click the Create account link and you will be able to access your OneDrive account.

NOTE *The OneDrive is linked directly to the email associated with the Microsoft account and it requires only a password to access. You should consider this in both setting the level of security on your password (i.e., the password complexity and length) and the type of files that you add to your OneDrive since password security is relatively easy for attackers to bypass.*

ACTIVITY 2.1—THE ONEDRIVE INTERFACE

For this activity, you should create a Microsoft account if you have not yet done so. Using your account, login to the OneDrive using the Web interface at *www.OneDrive.com*. Explore the interface and identify the method for either creating a new file on the OneDrive from any of the Web apps available. You do not need experience with the Office applications to do this successfully; you only need to create and save the file as practice. When prompted, save the file as *Activity2_1*.

2.2.2 Uploading and Downloading Files

When you enter your Microsoft account email and your associated password after your account has been verified, you will see the homepage for your OneDrive. You can see an example of this in Figure 2.2. This interface allows you to upload new files, manage files stored on your OneDrive account, and download files to the machine you are using.

In order to upload a file, just select the *Upload* link at the top of the interface. This opens a standard file selection interface for your OS where you can select the file you want to store on your OneDrive. Once you have chosen a

FIGURE 2.2 OneDrive Web interface

file, the upload will begin. The progress for this will be shown at the top of the interface, and an icon representing the file type (or a preview in the case of a photograph) will appear in your file list. Clicking on this icon will allow you to manage the file. This opens a context-sensitive set of options along the top of the interface, as shown in Figure 2.3. You can also right-click the icon to open a menu of options as well, which is also shown in Figure 2.3.

You can download the file from either the top interface's *Download* link or the right-click menu. You can share the file using the right-click menu and choosing *Share* or you can select *Manage* and then select the *Share* option in the pane that opens. The Share menu allows you to get a link to the item to distribute yourself or choose recipients for the file and OneDrive will email them a link to the item. You can set permissions on the link for whether you want them to have editing capabilities or not. The file properties will show you the share settings for the file.

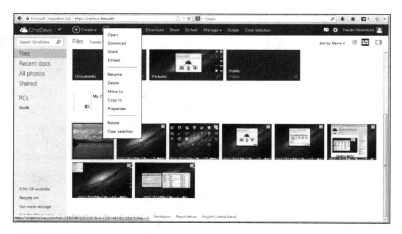

FIGURE 2.3 File management in OneDrive

NOTE *You can also use the Create icon to access the Web app versions of Word, PowerPoint, and Excel. This will create a new document and save it to your OneDrive account for later use. The Web apps will be discussed later with the respective application, but in general they are more condensed versions of the standalone software with only the core functionality.*

ACTIVITY 2.2—UPLOADING FILES

For this activity, you should login to the OneDrive using the Web interface at *www.OneDrive.com*. You should then choose a file from your desktop to upload to your OneDrive. You should not choose anything that contains sensitive or personal information. When you have selected the file, upload it to your OneDrive. Using the options available in the Share settings, create a link to the file. Paste the link in another tab or window in your Web browser. What happens when you visit the link? What options do you have to set the permissions on the file from your OneDrive interface?

2.3 INTEGRATING ONEDRIVE WITH THE DESKTOP

In addition to the Web application for OneDrive, you can integrate OneDrive into your OS desktop environment for easier interaction. This will allow you to place files to be uploaded into the OneDrive folder and it will synchronize the contents with your OneDrive account as you specify. The integration process is slightly different for each OS, as described in the following sections.

2.3.1 OneDrive on Windows 7

When you install Microsoft Office 2013 on your Windows machine, it will install OneDrive Pro 2013 which allows you to set the URL for your OneDrive library which will synchronize with the application. You can also install the Microsoft OneDrive application from *http://windows.microsoft.com/en-us/ OneDrive/download#apps*. This will allow you to use your OneDrive just like any other folder on your OS, as shown in Figure 2.4.

You can connect your OneDrive Web application to your PC to allow you to access any files from your PC as long as it is turned on and connected to the Internet. This is a risk depending upon the type of information that you store on your computer since the security of the connection is only as strong as your OneDrive password. It is safer not to enable this option, but it does provide a convenience if you do allow it.

2.3.2 OneDrive on Windows 8

In addition to the installed standalone application for OneDrive that is available on Windows 7, a Windows 8 app version of OneDrive is available for use as well. This can be downloaded from the Windows 8 app store and it will

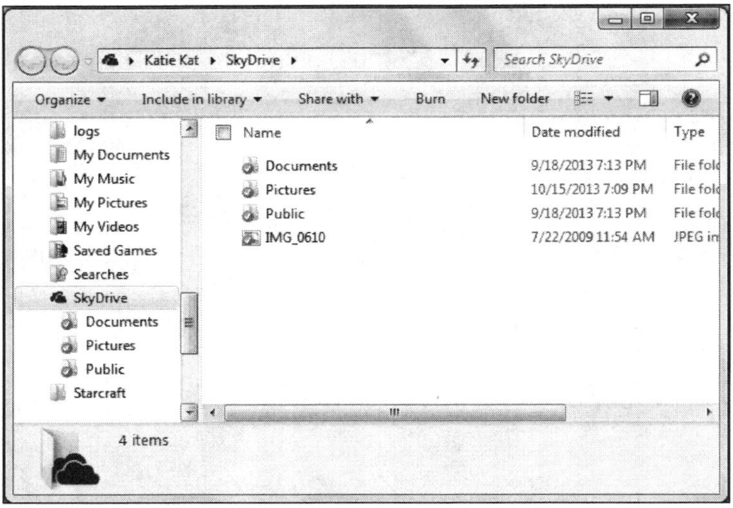

FIGURE 2.4 OneDrive integration in Windows 7

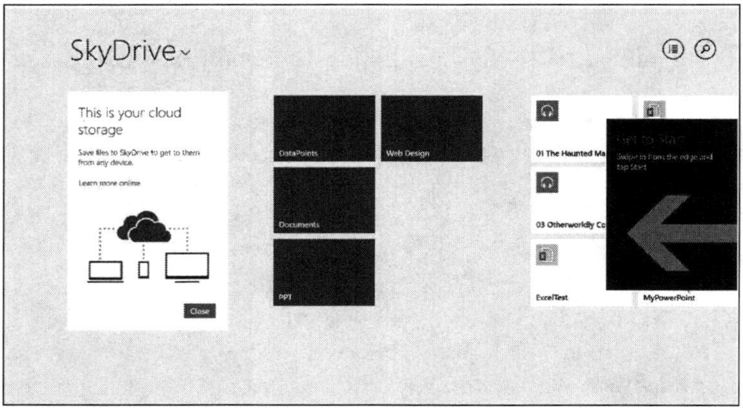

FIGURE 2.5 Windows 8 OneDrive app

appear in the Start screen. The interface for this app is shown in Figure 2.5. It functions similarly to the Web app version and allows you to directly upload and download files to and from your OneDrive and your computer.

2.3.3 OneDrive on Mac OS X

OneDrive is also compatible with Mac OS X. To add OneDrive to your Mac, open the App Store and search for "OneDrive." This will allow you to install the application on your system and add an icon for managing the OneDrive to your Dock. The application will create a folder on your system that is connected to your OneDrive. This folder acts like any other but it uploads the contents to your OneDrive account. You can see an example of the Dock icon and the OneDrive application in action on a Mac in Figure 2.6.

FIGURE 2.6 Mac OS X OneDrive icon and connected folder

ACTIVITY 2.3—INTEGRATING ONEDRIVE

For this activity, you should install OneDrive on your OS. Using a different file or the same file from the previous activity, you should place a file in the OneDrive folder that is now present in your OS. Revisit your OneDrive through the Web interface after a few moments (long enough for the file to upload). Does the file appear? How is it organized within your OneDrive account? Practice the process of downloading the file from the OneDrive Web interface to your desktop.

2.4 INTEGRATING ONEDRIVE WITH MICROSOFT OFFICE

Microsoft Office 2013 has direct integration with a Microsoft account and the OneDrive. When you sign into your Microsoft account with any Office program, the OneDrive becomes available as a storage location to open or save files from the File menu, just like any other folder on your machine. This is supported by all of the primary productivity programs: Word, Excel, and PowerPoint. When you sign into your Microsoft account on one of the Office programs, the account will be saved for the rest of the Office suite as well for whenever you open a different program.

To sign into a Microsoft account from a Microsoft Office application, such as Word, select the *File* menu and choose the *Account* option. This will open a screen similar to Figure 2.7. Choosing *Sign In* will prompt you to enter your Microsoft account email address and password.

When you have successfully signed into your Microsoft account, you can change the appearance of your programs, including the theme and background. You can also choose the *Add a service* option to connect to your OneDrive to use it as a storage location directly from the File menu.

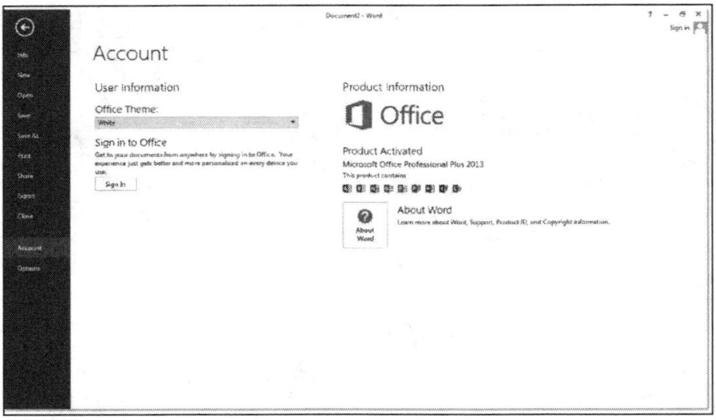

FIGURE 2.7 Account settings in Office 2013

FIGURE 2.8 Account options in Office 2013

When you return to your document or file, you will see your name in the right corner of the interface. You can click on your name to open a dropdown box with account options as shown in Figure 2.9. This is primarily cosmetic in appearance aside from the use of the OneDrive for storing and retrieving files.

ACTIVITY 2.4—SAVING A FILE TO THE ONEDRIVE

Using the program that you opened to add your account, save the file you created to your preferred document location. Using either the integrated OneDrive location or the folder you established on your OS, save the file to your OneDrive. Connect to the OneDrive and open the file from the remote location. What options are provided to you for opening the document? Is there another way to open the document in the desktop application? How is this beneficial?

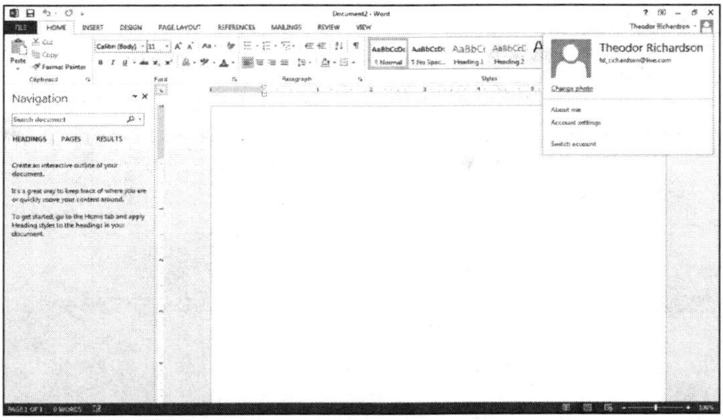

FIGURE 2.9 Account menu in Word 2013

2.5 ACCESSING ONEDRIVE ON A REMOTE DEVICE

OneDrive is also available for iOS and Android mobile devices. It is located in the iTunes app store for iOS devices like the iPhone and iPad, and it can be found in the Google Play store for Android. In both cases, it can be found by searching for "OneDrive" in the search box. When installed, it allows you to access the features of OneDrive for managing and sharing your files. The login for this is the same as accessing the Web interface; you simply use your Microsoft account and the password you selected.

NOTE *OneDrive is the only common cloud service that is available to use on a Windows smart phone.*

The mobile versions are primarily for managing and viewing photos and videos, but you can download documents for use in other programs. The upload and sharing features are optimized for the smaller screen in both of these versions so it will work efficiently with a smart phone.

2.6 ALTERNATE CLOUD COMPUTING PLATFORMS

Microsoft is not the only company that provides free cloud storage. However, if you use Office in any significant way, it does have the advantage of integrating with that software system and provides you with a Web app interface that should be familiar. Different companies have different benefits and services associated with their cloud storage. Some cloud computing systems cost money to use but may provide a higher level of security or a higher storage capacity. Some of these charge on a monthly basis while others are free. The two alternatives that most closely reflect the purpose and use of OneDrive are Google Drive and iCloud by Apple.

2.6.1 Google Drive

Similar to the relationship between OneDrive and a Microsoft account, Google Drive is automatically enabled for free with a Google account. Google Drive provides 15 GB of free storage as well as separate access to the Google productivity apps for creating new word processing, spreadsheet, and presentation documents. Google Drive can be similarly integrated into most computing environments, but it is focused primarily on document storage and transfer. Google Drive is not optimized for sharing photos and videos.

2.6.2 iCloud

iCloud is Apple's cloud computing platform. It is included in their OS by default. It allows for 5 GB of free storage for certain file types, like photographs. If you want to store additional file types, you need to purchase other software like iWork. iCloud is accessible on PCs as well as remote devices through a control interface that allows for file upload and download, similar to other cloud services. Additional storage space is available for purchase.

CHAPTER SUMMARY

This chapter covered the basics of cloud computing, primarily for storing and retrieving files remotely. Microsoft OneDrive was covered more extensively for its integration into the Microsoft Office suite and the access it provides to the Web app versions of the common Office productivity applications. OneDrive integrates directly with Office 2013 as a direct storage location and it is supported on Mac and Windows computers. The next chapter will begin the main coverage of productivity software with Microsoft Office.

CHAPTER KNOWLEDGE CHECK

1. The Microsoft OneDrive can be accessed on _____.
   a. The Web
   b. A Windows desktop
   c. An iPad
   d. All of the above
   e. None of the above
   f. a and b

2. Files on the OneDrive can be unshared, meaning the account owner is the only one who can access the file.
   a. True
   b. False

3. Only certain file types can be uploaded to the OneDrive.
   a. True
   b. False

4. The OneDrive provides _____ GB of storage space for free.
   a. 2
   b. 5
   c. 15
   d. None of the above

5. Connecting your Microsoft account to the Office applications allows you to _____.
   a. Customize the interface of the Office applications
   b. Save files to the OneDrive
   c. Store the Office application in the cloud so it can be used anywhere
   d. All of the above
   e. None of the above
   f. a and b

PRACTICE EXERCISES

1. Use the Web interface for the OneDrive to create a new Word document. Save the file to your OneDrive using the menus available. Create a link to share the document. Explain the different options that you have for sharing the document. When would each one be used? Give examples to support your answer.

2. Upload a picture to your OneDrive and open it in the Web interface. If you do not have one of your own, you can use the Web to locate an image that you may use. What options are presented which are unique to images? In your own words, explain why the mobile versions of the OneDrive are optimized for image and video sharing.

3. Use the desktop version of OneDrive to upload a file to your account. Download the file using the Web interface. Explain the steps that it took to complete this cycle. Complete the process in reverse, uploading the file through the Web interface. Does the uploaded file appear in the OneDrive folder on your desktop? How does the process differ for this path?

4. Using the Web, explain briefly why passwords are not the highest level of security. How should this influence the material that you connect to your OneDrive? What consequences would arise if all of the files on your entire computer were accessible on your OneDrive account?

CHAPTER 3

INTRODUCTION TO POWERPOINT AND PRESENTATION SOFTWARE

In This Chapter

This chapter is an introduction to presentation software and basic steps in constructing a presentation. You will create, edit, and save a simple presentation while learning to use the common tools required for developing professional presentations, such as text formatting and using templates. Once you have completed the chapter, you will be able to:

- Navigate the interface for Microsoft PowerPoint
- Locate and use the File menu for most applications
- Access the help files for an application
- Insert and format text in a presentation presentation

3.1 INTRODUCTION TO PRESENTATION SOFTWARE

In the past, lecturers, business leaders, researchers, teachers, and anyone wishing to present an idea had to construct their own visual aids on paper or chalkboards to supplement their oral presentations. This was time consuming and generally was not easily transferrable to another venue. Technology like slide projectors and overhead projectors made this process easier, but it still carried a significant development requirement to produce the slides or the overhead sheets. Presentation software is the digital equivalent to these analog technologies and lowers the barrier to creating effective visual supplements to any presentation.

Presentation software is a common component of most productivity software packages. Microsoft Office is an example of a software suite that is used for productivity. A *software suite* is a collection of individual programs that are used to perform related tasks; in the case of Office, this is the management of presentations for creating documents, presentations, spreadsheets, and email. An example of presentation software is Microsoft PowerPoint, which comes with the Microsoft Office suite.

> *Productivity software* is a program that assists you in performing tasks that are necessary for you to accomplish at home or in the workplace. Productivity is a measurement of how much you can accomplish in a given period of time.

The native format for PowerPoint is the presentation, and it takes the form of a slide show. Slide shows are primarily a visual supplement to an oral presentation, although they can also be used as a standalone slide show playing in the background of an event or as a demonstration that can be shared or posted on the Web. A critical thing to remember is that presentation software is not useful for a large volume of written text; that belongs in word processing software. Any text contained in a presentation should be short and to the point (the power point, if you will).

> *Presentation software* is a computer program that typically runs on a personal computer and allows the user to create visual aids, handouts, and graphics that may include sound and animation.

Office has different versions depending on which operating system you have on your computer. Office 2013 is the most current version for a Windows machine, and Office 2011 is the most current version for a Macintosh. Both versions allow for the completion of nearly identical tasks. Office also includes an online app version of the software for use with a Windows Live account; this version does not require a license to use but it does not have the full functionality associated with the full version of the software.

> *If you do not already have Office installed on your machine, you can get a trial version of the 2013 software for Windows from the Office homepage at* www.office.com. *For the 2011 version of the Office software for Macintosh, go to* www.microsoft.com/mac.

NOTE *Companies like JourneyEd (*www.journeyed.com*) offer discounted professional software to students. If you are using another site to get a discount on your software, remember that whenever you purchase software from a source other than the official vendor, you should make sure the site is legitimate before you attempt to make a purchase or enter any personal information. This is part of being a responsible Web user.*

For the most part, there is little difference in functionality between the Office 2013 and Office 2011 versions of the program. The differences are mainly in the placement of commands between the two versions, and these will be pointed out in the text as you follow along with the examples. You access the programs that are part of Office on a Windows 7 machine by selecting the *Start* menu, choosing *All Programs*, and then choosing *Microsoft Office 2013*; you will then see a listing of programs from which to choose. For this you want to choose *Microsoft PowerPoint*. If you are using Windows 8, the Start screen should contain an icon for PowerPoint once the program is installed. You can see the PowerPoint icon for Windows in Figure 3.1.

FIGURE 3.1 PowerPoint shortcut icon in Windows

To access Office 2011 on the Macintosh, you may be able to click the icons installed on the Dock (when you installed the software, you probably had the option to place the shortcut icons there). If you do not have the icons on your Dock, you can access the programs in the Office 2011 suite by selecting *Macintosh HD* (or whatever name you have given your machine) from the desktop, opening the *Applications* folder, and then opening the *Microsoft Office 2011* folder. Select *Microsoft PowerPoint* from the available programs.

NOTE *Whenever you activate one of the Office programs on a Macintosh, you will first be presented with a gallery of options for selecting templates or existing presentations. You can simply select* Cancel *on this screen to get to the standard interface.*

3.1.1 The File Menu

The *File* menu and the help files should be the first items you locate in any new software system. The *File* menu exists in almost all software applications written today and enables you to perform the essential tasks of creating a new file, opening an existing file, saving a file, printing a file, and exiting the program. While there may be additional options available in the File menu, these basic tasks warrant further investigation. The File menu is typically located at the left side of the software interface. Figure 3.2 shows the File menu for PowerPoint. In PowerPoint 2013, the File menu (which is also called the Backstage view in the Office

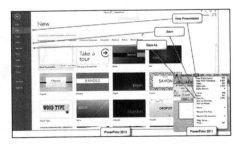

FIGURE 3.2 File menu in PowerPoint

2013 suite) is found to the far left on the ribbon interface. In PowerPoint 2011, it is located beside the Apple menu at the top of the computer screen.

There are several essential commands found within the File menu with which you should become familiar:

- *New*—The New command is used to create a new file of the type associated with the program. In the case of PowerPoint, this file is a presentation. The

New command may present you with several alternatives if the program supports different presentation types or presentation creation options.

- *Save As*—This command opens a dialog box to allow you to select the name, file type, and location to which you would like your file stored; this operates on the file that is currently active in the program. If you have already saved your presentation and want to save a copy or save it with a different name, you can do so with this option. For PowerPoint, the default file type is *PowerPoint Presentation* (*.pptx*), but there are several alternative file types available when saving a presentation including *Portable Document Format* (*.pdf*). It is important to use Save As to save a new file you have created so your work will not be lost if there is a problem with the software system or you close it by accident. The Save As dialog box for PowerPoint is shown in Figure 3.3. PowerPoint 2013 will provide you with a list of commonly used folders where you can store your work; if you do not see the folder where you wish to store your file, you can always click the *Browse* icon in the right column of the interface to select any location on your machine.

- *Save*—The Save command allows you to save the file that you currently have open within the software application; this is useful for making sure your recent changes are retained in the presentation. The first time you save the presentation after it is created, this command will typically function like the Save As command.

- *Open*—The Open command is used to reopen existing presentations. Selecting this command opens a dialog box that is similar to the one used to save presentations and allows you to select a presentation from the current folder on the right-hand side of the dialog box. You can also type the name of the file you want to open in the File Name field, and any files that are a match to the partial string you have typed will appear in a box as options to select. Similar to the Save As functionality, PowerPoint 2013 will provide you with a list of commonly used folders where you can open your work as well as a list of recent files in the rightmost column; if you do not see the folder or file you wish to open, you can always click the *Browse* icon in the right column of the interface to select any location on your machine.

- *Print*—This command allows you to send the current file to an installed printer. Printing requires additional hardware and a driver installation for that hardware to work. In Office 2013, you are given a software-based print option of *Send to OneNote 2013* as a possible printer regardless of what other printers you have installed. If you have installed Ado-

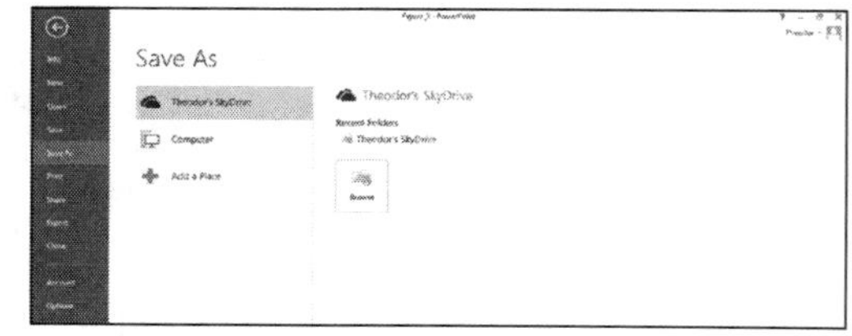

FIGURE 3.3 Save As dialog box in PowerPoint

be Acrobat® Professional, you will also get the software-based option of printing to a *Portable Document Format (.pdf)* file.

- *Exit or Close*—Selecting this command will close the program. On a Macintosh, closing the windows of the program will not exit the program entirely; you must select the *File* menu and choose *Exit* to fully close the program. On Windows, selecting Close will terminate the program unless there are other instances of it open for other presentations. In this case, all presentation windows must be closed to fully exit the program.

ACTIVITY 3.1—SAVING AND OPENING FILES

You should practice saving and opening presentations to see how the creating presentations software interacts with the file system of the operating system. If you have not done so, you should create a folder called *Activities* somewhere on your computer (this should be located somewhere in your presentation libraries or inside your My Documents folder where you can locate it easily). You should already have your initial file (that opened by default when you started the program) which you should save as MyNewPresentation. Create a new presentation and save it (using the default file extension selected in the dialog box) as *Activity3_1*. Close these two files and then open them again. If your software application closes when you close these files, as in the case of the Windows version which closes when there are no open presentations, you should start it again from the operating system. By the end of this activity, you should have both *MyNewPresentation* and *Activity3_1* open again.

3.1.2 Presentation File Management

Whenever you are working on a project, it is important to manage the files associated with that project. You have already learned about using folders in previous chapters. Throughout the rest of this text, you will be creating projects in every chapter. You should be sure to keep your work organized—not just for the purposes of learning but also for the general management of productivity. If you already have a designated folder for your projects, you should create a new folder within it and title the folder *Presentations*. It is a good idea to create folders to manage your different responsibilities so you can find items when you need them; the same rules that apply to filing and sorting paper presentations also apply to organizing electronic presentations.

- There are several options for saving your files from PowerPoint. The default file type for the PowerPoint application is PowerPoint Presentation which has a file extension of *.pptx*. This is selected by default when you save the presentation. You can also use the compatibility format for PowerPoint presentations so that the presentations you create can be viewed in older versions of PowerPoint without issues; this presentation format is called PowerPoint 97-03 and has the presentation extension *.ppt*. Using the *.ppt* file format disables the new features of PowerPoint but preserves backward compatibility with prior versions; the need for this is becoming less common since the 2007 and 2008 versions of PowerPoint also used the new *.pptx* format and features. In addition to these options, you can also save your presentation from the PowerPoint application in other file formats:

- A Portable Document Format (PDF) file (which uses a *.pdf* extension) is constructed from printing commands and it produces a static presentation that cannot be edited or reformatted without specialized software. Unlike the native PowerPoint file format, which can change depending on the software version and installed fonts, there is no variance in the display of a PDF file (a format that was invented by the Adobe company). This means it will display for the viewer exactly as you intend it to be seen. You can create a PDF file of your PowerPoint presentation by selecting PDF as the file type in the Save As dialog box in both PowerPoint 2013 and PowerPoint 2011. The most common application for viewing *PDF* files is the Adobe Reader, which is available in a free version from *www.adobe.com* (by typing "Adobe Reader" in the search box).
- The XML Paper Specification (XPS) format is the Microsoft version of a PDF; this type of file requires a special viewer for the application type but it has the same fixed display property of the PDF presentation. The presentation extension for this type of file is *.xps*.
- PowerPoint can also export a slide or an entire presentation as images or video. There are a number of different formats available for this type of export. When you save a presentation in this format, it does not save any changes that were made to your presentation in the native PowerPoint format.

ACTIVITY 3.2—FILE TYPES

Now that you have an understanding of the different types of file formats that are available for saving a presentation from PowerPoint, you should create a new presentation and save it using the default file format as *Activity3_2*. You should add a line of text to the presentation such as "This is my new presentation." Now, save the presentation in the folder for this chapter in each of the following file formats: PDF, XPS, and JPG File Interchange Format. Depending on the type of file format you select, you may need to re-open the original presentation to save it in a new format. What are the application icons for each of these formats that appear as the default program to open them?

3.1.3 Help Files

Help files are almost always included in a software system. These files allow you to get definitions of elements in the software system and obtain help in performing common tasks and troubleshooting. On a Windows machine, pressing the *F1* key will activate the Help interface for whatever program you currently have selected (if you are using the operating system when you press

FIGURE 3.4 PowerPoint Help interface in PowerPoint

F1, you will open the help interface for the operating system). On a Macintosh, the Help interface is available by selecting the *Help* menu at the top of the screen; this will be context-sensitive for the program you have active. The PowerPoint Help interface is shown in Figure 3.4. Most help files, including those in Office, allow you to search for entries using a keyword search.

3.1.4 Productivity Shortcuts

Productivity shortcuts are keyboard commands that can be entered quickly to save you the time of having to open a menu or ribbon to find the command you wish to use. These exist for the most common actions you perform in a software system and are common to most software programs that utilize individual presentations or files to store and organize information.

You activate a shortcut command by holding down the *Ctrl* key on a Windows machine and typing the letter corresponding to the shortcut while the *Ctrl* key is held down. These shortcuts work on a Macintosh machine as well, except the *Command* key is used to activate the shortcut instead of the *Ctrl* key. The most common shortcuts with which you should be familiar are as follows:

- *New Presentation* (*Ctrl-N* on Windows machines or *Command-N* on Macintosh machines)—This command opens a new blank presentation in the active program.
- *Open Presentation* (*Ctrl-O* or *Command-O*)—This is used to open an existing file. It will open a dialog box that allows you to choose the file you wish to open.
- *Save Presentation* (*Ctrl-S* or *Command-S*)—This is the same as selecting the Save command; it will save any progress in an open presentation that has already been saved. If the presentation has not yet been saved, it will act like the Save As command.
- *Print Document* (*Ctrl-P* or *Command-P*)—This command initiates the printing process. If the software allows you to set options before you print, it will open a dialog box; otherwise, it will attempt to use the default printer to initiate a print command.
- *Undo Last Action* (*Ctrl-Z* or *Command-Z*)—This will attempt to undo the last action you performed in the open presentation; not all actions can be undone with this command. Some programs maintain a buffer of actions, allowing you to undo multiple changes that you made to the presentation.
- *Redo Last Action* (*Ctrl-Y* or *Command-Y*)—This will reverse the effects of the Undo command; not all actions that are undone can be reversed by

the Redo command. Again, there are some programs that will maintain a buffer of commands and changes, allowing you to redo multiple actions that were reversed by the Undo command.

- *Select All Content (Ctrl-A or Command-A)*—This command will select all of the content in the current presentation or presentation element (like a table cell) that is allowed to be selected. This is a useful command if you want to perform actions like applying formatting to everything in your presentation.
- *Quit (Ctrl-Q or Command-Q)*—This command will attempt to exit the currently active program.

There are additional shortcuts that are used often to utilize the system clipboard for transferring information quickly and easily from one presentation or location to another. These are valuable to learn and will save you a considerable amount of time when you are typing. There are also shortcuts to common formatting changes that will be discussed later in this chapter as you start your first project in creating presentations. Additionally, specific programs may have a unique set of shortcut commands in addition to or instead of the ones covered here.

3.1.5 The System Clipboard

The system clipboard is temporary storage for anything you copy from a presentation or folder that allows you to use it again elsewhere. When you copy an object or a grouping of text to the clipboard, all of its formatting and content are retained. The copied material can then be pasted in another location in any of the productivity software programs. For instance, you can copy formatted text from Word and paste it into PowerPoint and it will retain any formatting that was applied to it. Similarly, you can copy a chart from Excel and paste it into a PowerPoint presentation. This interoperability and the ease of use of the clipboard make it a valuable tool for productivity.

The three commands that apply to the clipboard are:

- *Copy*—The Copy command is used to make a duplicate of selected text or objects in a presentation. Copy will leave the original source of the material intact in the presentation and make a duplicate on the clipboard. The Copy icon looks like two sheets of paper overlapping each other. The shortcut for the Copy command is *Ctrl-C* on a Windows machine and *Command-C* on a Macintosh machine.
- *Cut*—The Cut command functions like Copy except it removes the original source material from the presentation (whether it is text or an object) and places it on the clipboard. The Cut icon is traditionally a pair of scissors; the shortcut for the Cut command is *Ctrl-X* on a Windows machine and *Command-X* on a Macintosh machine.
- *Paste*—The Paste command is used to place the contents of the clipboard at the active cursor location within a selected presentation. Whether the

contents are then removed from the clipboard depends on the specific program; in PowerPoint, they are not removed and can be pasted multiple times. The Paste icon looks like either a clipboard or a bottle of rubber cement (which was traditionally used to place clippings of presentations in other presentations). The shortcut for Paste is *Ctrl-V* on Windows and *Command-V* on Macintosh.

If you copy formatted text from one presentation and paste it into a presentation location that does not allow formatting, such as Notepad on a Windows machine, the text will be pasted and the formatting will be removed. The spacing of the letters (such as blank space characters created using the spacebar or tab indents from the Tab key) will be retained to match the way the keys and spacing are defined in the target presentation. This can actually be helpful for removing unwanted formatting from Web presentations or PDF files.

3.2 ANATOMY OF MICROSOFT POWERPOINT

Whenever you open PowerPoint from a menu or from a desktop icon, a new presentation (typically named *Presentation1*) will open. To create a new presentation in PowerPoint 2013, select the *File* menu and then select *New*. A list of presentation templates from which you can create your presentation will appear. Select *Blank Presentation* and either double-click the icon or click the *Create* button. You can also use the *Ctrl-N* shortcut to create a new presentation with the default settings.

In PowerPoint 2011, select the *File* menu and then choose *New Presentation*, or use the shortcut *Command-N*. You can also create a new presentation from an existing template under the File menu, but for now you should just create a new blank presentation.

Remember that Microsoft Office 2013 (including PowerPoint 2013) is the latest version available for the Windows operating system. Microsoft Office 2011 (including PowerPoint 2011) is the latest version available for the Macintosh operating system. These versions are both included in the Office 365 subscription service.

NOTE

Whenever you are working on a presentation, it is imperative to save often. You should always start saving when the presentation is first created. With your new *Presentation1* (the default file) open, click *File* to open the interface for the file options. On the main list in the open menu, you have the Save and Save As options. Save will attempt to save the presentation to an existing location, but if you have not yet saved the presentation, it will act like Save As.

Now you should be at the main slide of your new presentation. PowerPoint has an interface that is very similar to Word. A few of the ribbons contain almost identical tools. PowerPoint is designed for visualization, so the ability to format text and insert media quickly is the essential element that distinguishes

PowerPoint from the rest of the Office suite. When you look at the default interface, you will see the initial *title* slide and the available ribbons and commands. A quick tour of the interface is provided first and then you will learn the steps to creating a successful presentation. The interfaces for PowerPoint 2013 and PowerPoint 2011 are slightly different, so feel free to jump to the section that is relevant to you. The Microsoft PowerPoint Web App is also available for anyone with a OneDrive account. Just like the other app versions of the Office programs, the PowerPoint Web App is limited in functionality compared to the full installation versions.

3.2.1 Microsoft PowerPoint 2013

Along the top of the PowerPoint 2013 interface (which is shown in Figure 3.5) is a series of icons that act as quick commands; this is the Quick Access toolbar. The PowerPoint icon itself contains a short list of commands that allow you to move and change the size of your interface window.

Clicking the icon that looks like a floppy disk lets you save your presentation quickly after you have made changes (it acts like the Save command, but if you have never saved your presentation it will act as the Save As command).

By default, the Quick Access toolbar also has the Undo command to erase the effects of your last action as though it had never happened; the drop-down arrow beside the icon opens a menu of several prior actions and lets you select how many of them you want to undo. The Redo command allows you to redo what you undid. These two icons allow you to step forward and backward through your changes in case you made a mistake along the way.

On the right side at the top of the interface are icons to minimize, maximize, and close your presentation (make sure you save before you click this button) and an icon to access the help files. Beneath these icons, there is an arrow to show or hide your ribbons. The first ribbon beside the File button is the Home ribbon. From here, you can insert new slides, modify text, insert quick drawing elements, arrange items, and find and replace text in the presentation.

The main departure from PowerPoint you will encounter here is that PowerPoint is arranged into slides and sections instead of pages. To insert a slide, either click the *New Slide* command on the *Home* ribbon or right-click the *Slides/Outline* pane on the left side of the interface. When you select the *New Slide* command, you can choose the type of layout you want for the slide you are inserting. If you use the right-click option, you will get a new slide with the default layout.

The *Insert* ribbon, shown in Figure 3.6, is the next one in line. You will visit this ribbon a lot if you plan to work frequently with media, which is really the main purpose

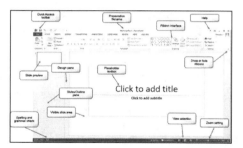

FIGURE 3.5 Anatomy of PowerPoint 2013

FIGURE 3.6 Insert ribbon in PowerPoint 2013

of using PowerPoint. From this ribbon, you can insert just about anything you can imagine, from text boxes and pictures to clip art and equations, not to mention sounds and videos. You can try it out by clicking *Shapes* in the *Illustrations* panel. Select a shape you like and place it into your slide. If you select a shape and just click on the slide, a predefined instance of the shape will be stamped into the slide. You can also click and drag to set the size of the shape yourself.

The next ribbon is the *Design* ribbon, shown in Figure 3.7; this is where you can select how you want your presentation to look. Go ahead and select something from the *Themes* panel. Notice how doing so reformats your text and recolors any shapes that you did not modify. Each theme has a set color scheme and font choice, but you can change these using the *Colors and Fonts* menus; each of these has a drop-down list of predefined selections from which you can choose. You can also change the default effects that are applied to shapes within the presentation by clicking on *Effects. The Background* panel lets you change a number of settings, but for now select how you want your background to appear from a preset drop-down list of options under *Background Styles*. These will change based on the overall theme you have selected. Your presentation is starting to look fancy already!

The next ribbon to consider at this point is the *Slide Show* ribbon, shown in Figure 3.8. The *Slide Show* ribbon is useful for previewing how your slide show will look when it is presented. On the *Start Slide Show* panel, you can select either *From Beginning* or *From Current Slide* to start your show. Select *From Beginning*. You can also start your slide show from the beginning by pressing F5 on your keyboard.

You should now be in the *Slide Show* view; this is the view you will use whenever you are presenting. It resets your slides to the full size of the screen and hides the design interface of the software. You can move forward in your slides by clicking the mouse, pressing the spacebar, the enter key, or using the right arrow key. You can move backward through your presentation by using the left arrow key. When you get to the end of your show, moving the presentation forward will display a black screen that says "End of slide show. Click to exit." Moving the presentation forward from this slide will take you out of the presentation mode and back into the *Normal* view you use for creation. You can also end the slide show at any time by pressing the *Escape* key.

FIGURE 3.7 Design ribbon in PowerPoint 2013

FIGURE 3.8 Slide Show ribbon in PowerPoint 2013

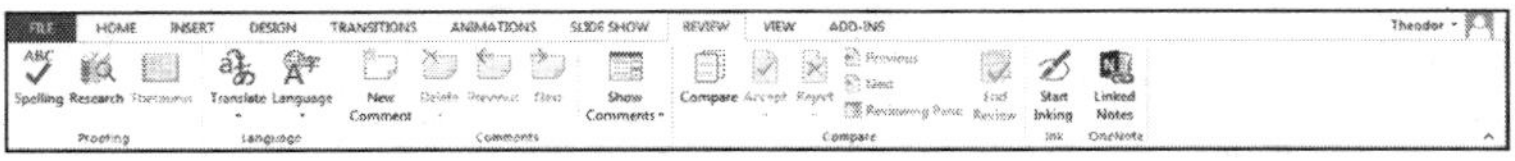

FIGURE 3.9 Review ribbon in PowerPoint 2013

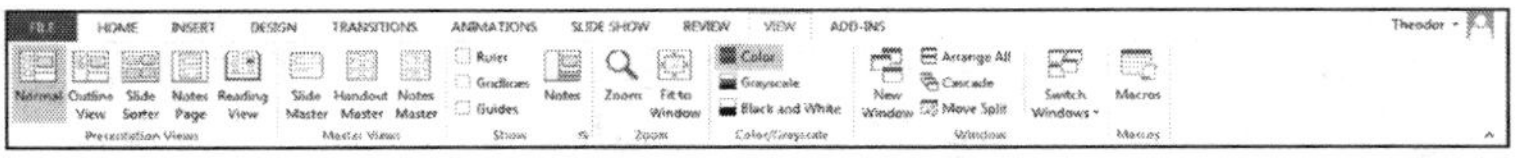

FIGURE 3.10 View ribbon in PowerPoint 2013

The *Review* ribbon, shown in Figure 3.9, is similar to the one found in PowerPoint. You can use the *Proofing* panel to check spelling for your entire presentation, find research references, and use the thesaurus to find alternate words. You can also set your language preferences from this ribbon. Go ahead and click the *Spelling* icon. You should have no errors if you have not yet typed content into the slides! To run a check of spelling at any time, you can press the *Spelling and Grammar Check* icon at the bottom of the interface; the icon status will indicate if errors are found (an *X* will appear in this case).

The *View* ribbon, shown in Figure 3.10, is where you customize the user interface for PowerPoint and format your slides. You can also select your view and arrange your slides from this ribbon and edit the Slide Master for your presentation. The *Slide Master* is a parent of all of the individual slides in your presentation. Formatting changes made to the Slide Master will affect all of the existing and future slides in your presentation.

There is also an *Add-Ins* ribbon on your interface for any software that interacts with the Office suite. If you have Adobe Acrobat installed on your computer, you may also see a ribbon for that (called the *Acrobat* ribbon); this is an example of other programs that interoperate with the Office suite.

The largest portion of the interface is devoted to the current slide view. The left side of the interface contains the *Slides/Outline* pane, which allows you to preview your slides and navigate between them quickly. The bottom of the interface displays the slide count and several valuable quick links. You can toggle the display of the *Notes* pane from the bottom of the interface as well; these are notes that accompany the slide but do not display in the presentation.

You can select the view you want by clicking one of the view icons; this includes the *Normal* view for design, the *Slide Sorter* view for arranging your slides, and the *Slide Show* view for watching and presenting your slide show. Finally, you can shift the zoom percentage by moving the slide bar or fit your slide to the current window size by clicking the icon in the far-right corner. It is now time to go deeper into the software and start creating your first presentation.

3.2.2 Microsoft PowerPoint 2011

PowerPoint 2011 has a concise interface, shown in Figure 3.11, which is very similar to its PowerPoint 2013 counterpart. Aside from some placement differences for certain tools, almost all of the functionality of PowerPoint 2013 is mirrored in PowerPoint 2011 and vice versa. The main menu of the software

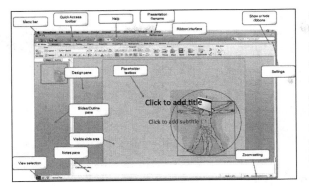

FIGURE 3.11 Anatomy of PowerPoint 2011

contains the *File* menu and a series of additional menus that provide shortcuts to commonly used tools, such as the *Insert* menu and the *Arrange* menu. The ribbons contain these functions as well, so it is up to you to decide your preferred method of accessing them.

The common icons to close, minimize, or maximize the presentation are directly beneath the main menu at the top of the free-floating window containing your presentation. As in all Mac software, clicking the close icon will exit your current presentation, but it will not quit the software; to do this, you must select the *PowerPoint* menu and then select *Quit PowerPoint*.

A *slide* was originally a small color transparency that was intended to be projected to a larger surface to assist in visualization. This term has been carried over to digital presentation software as the unit of the presentation, similar to a page in a text presentation.

The Quick Access toolbar for PowerPoint 2011 contains icons to allow you to save your work quickly, print your presentation, create a new presentation, open a presentation, and access help. There is also the *Undo* icon to allow you to undo any actions you made and the *Redo* icon to put back any changes you made with Undo. At the far right side of the interface is a text box to search your presentation for any keywords you enter.

The ribbon interface is directly beneath the Quick Access toolbar. The default ribbon is the *Home* ribbon, which contains tools to modify text, change fonts, and insert new elements into your slides. PowerPoint 2011 combines most of the functionality of the *Home* ribbon and the Insert ribbon from PowerPoint 2013 into its *Home* ribbon. The *New Slide* icon is at the far left of the *Home* ribbon; this is used to add slides to your presentation. The *Home* ribbon also contains the *Arrange* icon, which is used to arrange elements in your presentation; this will be visited often in the course of developing your presentation.

The next ribbon of interest is the *Themes* ribbon, shown in Figure 3.12. This is where you set the look and feel of your presentation. There are a number of preset options from which you can select. Go ahead and choose one that you like

FIGURE 3.12 Themes ribbon in PowerPoint 2011

and click on your selection to apply it to the presentation. The new theme will set defaults for the color, font, and background settings of your slides. You can make changes to these defaults at any time using the *Colors*, *Fonts*, and *Background* icons. There is a large selection of preset color schemes and font styles available; you can also use these menus to define your own.

The next several ribbons are used for more advanced functionality, so skip to the *Slide Show* ribbon, shown in Figure 3.13. This is used to set up your presentation views and timing for when you are presenting your slide show. Go ahead and click the *From Start* icon. This will put you into the *Slide Show* view, which is the view you will use to present your presentation to an audience. You can move your presentation forward by using the spacebar or the right arrow key and backward by using the left arrow key. To get out of *Slide Show* view and back to the *Normal* view used to design your slides, press the *Escape* key.

FIGURE 3.13 Themes ribbon in PowerPoint 2011

FIGURE 3.14 Review ribbon in PowerPoint 2011

The *Review* ribbon, shown in Figure 3.14, contains the functionality to compare versions of your presentation. It also allows you to add and delete comments in your slides and to set permissions for the presentation. Beneath the ribbon interface to the left is the *Slides/Outline* pane, which allows you to preview and quickly navigate to your slides by clicking on them. The main pane of the interface window is the slide *Design* pane. This contains the editable copy of your slide.

At the bottom of the interface, you can select your view via quick links; these include the *Normal* view for editing, the *Slide Sorter* view for arranging your slides, and the *Slide Show* view for watching or presenting your slide show. You can also adjust the zoom of your slides by changing the slide bar at the lower-right corner. Now that you have taken the tour of the software interface, you can start using the tools to construct your first presentation.

3.2.3 Microsoft PowerPoint Web App

PowerPoint is also available as a Web app on the OneDrive. From the homepage of OneDrive, click *Create* and then choose PowerPoint presentation. You will be prompted to choose the type of presentation you want (selecting "New blank presentation" is a good place to start for any presentation). The interface for the PowerPoint Web App is similar to the PowerPoint 2013 interface with less options and a fewer number of ribbons. You can see the interface for the PowerPoint Web App in Figure 3.15.

The *Home* ribbon for the PowerPoint Web app contains the formatting commands for text as well as a set of drawing objects that can be added to your presentation quickly. The *Insert* ribbon, which is shown in Figure 3.16, allows

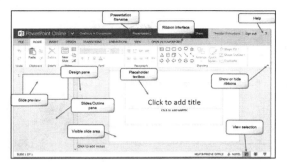

FIGURE 3.15 Anatomy of the PowerPoint Web App

you to add images, clip art, and the same illustration objects available from the *Home* ribbon. You can also add comments to a selected element from the *Insert* ribbon.

The *Design* ribbon allows you to select the theme you want for your presentation. You can also select variants from the theme for changing specific colors or other appearance elements once you have selected a theme. You can see the *Design* ribbon in Figure 3.17.

The *Animations* ribbon and *Transitions* ribbon control the more advanced functionality of PowerPoint. The *Transitions* ribbon will be covered later in this chapter, but animation is a more advanced topic. You can see these ribbons in Figure 3.18 for later reference.

The *View* ribbon allows you to change the view and to show or hide comments. The *Notes* pane is for adding notes to your slides for presenters or audience handouts. The *Reading* view shows only the content of the slide in the Internet browser, the *Normal* view shows the design interface, and the *Slide Show* view starts the slide show on your computer in full screen mode. You can see the *View* ribbon in Figure 3.19.

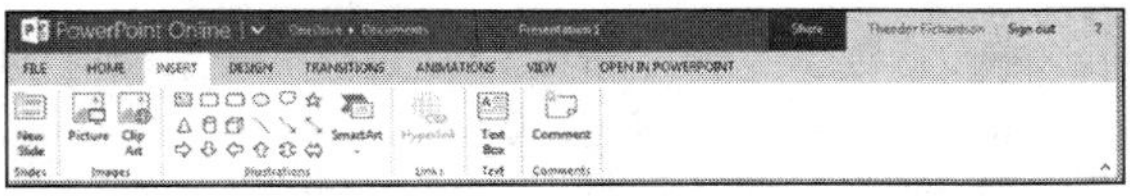

FIGURE 3.16 Insert ribbon in the PowerPoint Web App

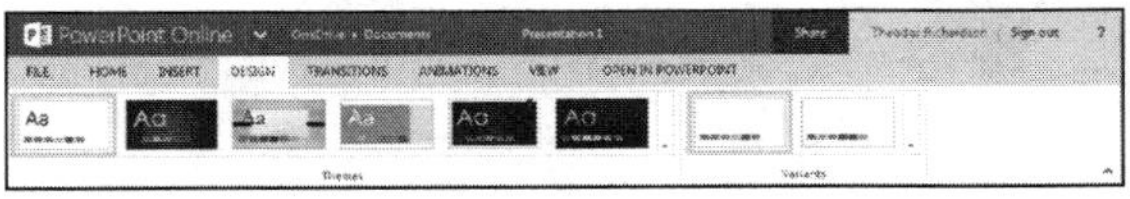

FIGURE 3.17 Design ribbon in the PowerPoint Web App

Note that there is no *Save* icon on the interface for the PowerPoint Web App because changes are saved as soon as an action is completed. The bottom of the interface has the toggle for opening and closing the Notes section and a selection of views. The ribbon interface also has the option to open the presentation in an installed version of PowerPoint on the host computer and the option to share your presentation using the *Share* icon.

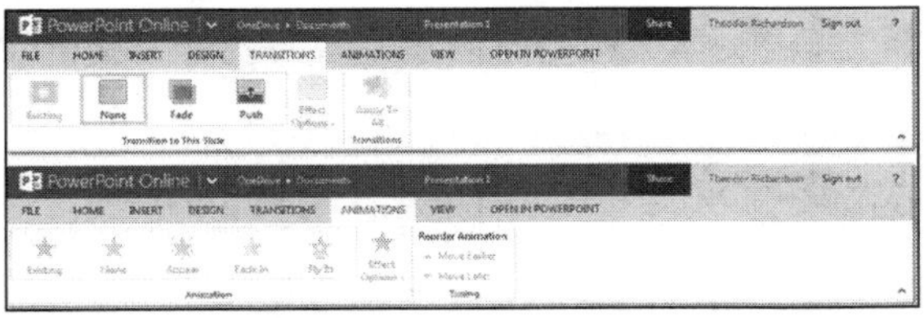

FIGURE 3.18 Transitions and Animations ribbons in the PowerPoint Web App

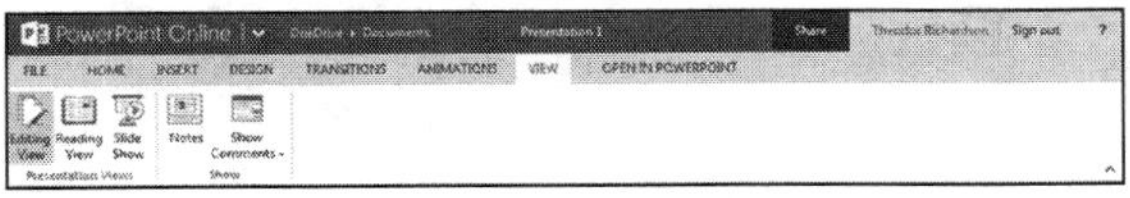

FIGURE 3.19 View ribbon in the PowerPoint Web App

3.3 DIVING INTO PRESENTATIONS

The first task in understanding PowerPoint is to be able to add slides and text and format both. Text formatting in PowerPoint works just like it does in Word if you have prior experience in that application. Instead of pages, a presentation uses slides. You can insert slides from the *Home* ribbon by clicking on *New Slide*. You can use the submenu of this icon or the options in the same panel to adjust the layout of the new slide you want to insert.

ACTIVITY 3.3—ADDING SLIDES

Create a new presentation and save it as *Activity3_3* in the *Activities* folder you created. Practice adding slides to your presentation. What are the different layout options for the slides that you add? What do each of these have in common and what is different for the layouts? Save your work.

3.3.1 Formatting Text

Text entry can be done in simpler programs like Notepad, as the real benefit of creating presentations or word processing software is the ability to format and change the appearance of text. The ability to design the appearance of your text, add additional media to your presentations, and share your presentations in multiple formats is where creating presentations stands out against simple text editors or word processing applications.

PowerPoint offers most of the same text effects as Microsoft Word. The differences are that there is no highlighting in PowerPoint and the Text Effects feature in PowerPoint 2013 is located on a separate, context-sensitive *Format* ribbon. Right-clicking on a text box activates a formatting menu with common links for text modification. You can see both of these in Figure 3.20.

Change the font of the text to something suitable and stylish and change the text to bold by clicking the *Bold* icon or pressing the *Ctrl-B* keys at the same time. Increase the font size by a single increment using the *Increase Font Size* icon. Note that you must select either the box surrounding the text or all of the text to apply your font changes to everything in the box; otherwise the changes will affect only the word in which the cursor is placed. You can change the size to a specific value with the drop-down box; this will accept a number (with or without a decimal point) as input, so you can define a size that is not part of the predefined selection options. Increase the font until the text covers most of the slide.

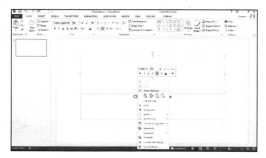

FIGURE 3.20 Format ribbon and right-click menu for text boxes

3.3.1.1 The Font Panel

The *Font* panel is common to most of the Office programs. This panel, located on the *Home* ribbon, contains the formatting commands for changing the font, size, style, and color of your text. The default font for a new presentation is Calibri (Body) on Windows and Cambria (Body) on the Macintosh. Select all of the text in your letter by using the *Select All* shortcut (*Ctrl-A* on Windows and *Command-A* on the Macintosh) and select *Times New Roman*.

A *font* is a complete set of keyboard characters in one particular style (the style is the name of the font). Most fonts support standard sizes as well as bold and italic variants.

The *Font* panel is shown in Figure 3.21. Remember that changes to the *Font* panel settings apply only to text that is selected when the changes are made. If no text is selected, the settings will be changed for text that is added at the current cursor location until another section of formatted text is encountered. By default, the format of new text that you enter will be consistent with the text immediately before it in the presentation.

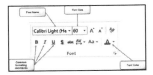

FIGURE 3.21 PowerPoint Font panel in the Home ribbon

You can change the size of your text (called the font size) in a number of ways: by selecting a preset value from the drop-down Font Size field, typing a number manually in the Font Size field, or using the *Grow Font* and *Shrink Font* icons to increment or decrement the size of the font. Select all of your text and change the font size to *12*. Font sizes are set in point values; a *point* is the smallest unit of measure in typography. There are 72 points per inch. An intermediate value called a *pica* is the equivalent of 12 points (so there are 6 picas per inch).

NOTE *There are several keyboard shortcuts for the common formatting enhancements. To bold text, use Ctrl-B (or Command-B on the Mac); to italicize text, use Ctrl-I (or Command-I); and to underline text, use Ctrl-U (or Command-U). These act as a toggle, so repeating the command will turn off the effect.*

You should take note of the styles that you can apply to your text in the *Font* panel. Bold, Italic, and Underline are all means of adding emphasis to your text. Bold will make the text thicker and darker, Italic will slant the text, and Underline will add a line under the text. Strikethrough retains the text but crosses it out; this is used to show completed tasks in a list of tasks. The strikethrough used to be an indicator of an error correction in typewritten presentations, but there is no need for this use in modern presentation software except for specific emphasis.

To change the color of the text itself, you use the *Font Color* icon. Clicking on the drop-down arrow opens a menu from which you can select any of the colors of the current theme setting and standard colors. You can also utilize custom colors or a gradient by selecting these options from the menu. Finally, using the *Clear Formatting* icon (which looks like an eraser) will remove any changes you have made to the formatting of the selected text and reset it to the default font settings for the presentation.

FIGURE 3.22 Font dialog box in PowerPoint 2013

In PowerPoint 2013, the expansion icon in the lower-right corner of the *Font* panel opens the *Font* dialog box. In PowerPoint 2011, you open the *Font* dialog box by selecting the Format menu and choosing *Font*. The *Font* dialog box is shown in Figure 3.22. This dialog box allows you to configure the font, size, effects, and enhancements for your text in a single interface.

3.3.1.2 The Paragraph Panel

The *Paragraph* panel is located beside the *Font* panel on the *Home* ribbon and is shown in Figure 3.23. This panel provides options for bullets and numbering, outline formatting, text indent (to increase or decrease indent), text alignment, and spacing between lines. Text alignment will be a bigger concern when you start adding complex vis-

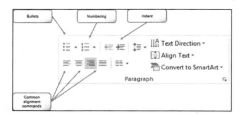

FIGURE 3.23 PowerPoint Paragraph panel in the Home ribbon

ual elements to your presentations. For now, though, use the *Align Text Right* icon to align text to the right margin of your text box. You will notice that the default setting is for text to be aligned to the left.

The *Line Spacing* icon allows you to select the number of lines of space given for each line of text (by default, this is set at 1.15 lines of space per line in the menu); this spacing is based on the font size of the text, so double spacing (two lines of space per line of text) for a 12 pt font will be equal to 24 pts of space, but for an 18 pt font will be 36 pts of space. There are also a few options for paragraph spacing. The *Paragraph* dialog box offers a more detailed selection of options for line spacing.

3.3.1.3 Format Painter

It is important to give any presentation you create a consistent look and feel. You will learn about managing styles in the coming chapters, but one way to provide consistency is to use format painting. This process takes the formatting modifications from the currently selected text or object and applies them to any text or object that is highlighted after you click the *Format Painter* icon. This icon, which looks like a paintbrush, is located in the *Home* ribbon in PowerPoint 2013 and in the Quick Access toolbar in PowerPoint 2011.

3.3.2 Bullets and Numbering

Bullet points are the primary text presentation tool for presentations. This allows you to make several short statements or have a few key phrases to supplement your verbal presentation. Adding text to any placeholder in a slide will automatically convert your items to an unordered list of elements. You can change the style of the bullet point by selecting from among the available options in the drop-down arrow menu for the *Bullets* icon, shown in Figure 3.24.

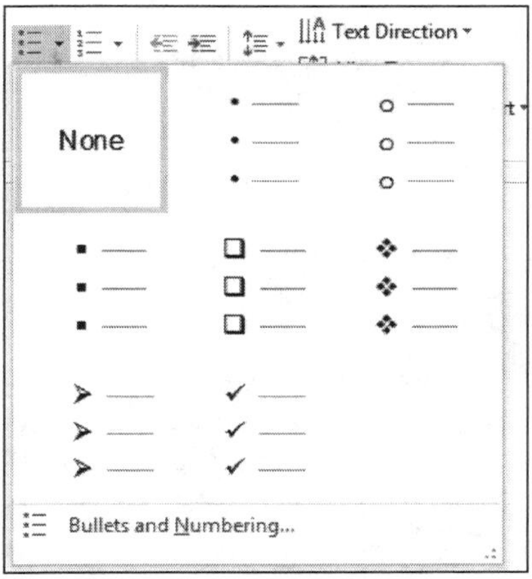

There are similar options available from the *Numbering* icon's drop-down arrow menu. The significant difference between numbering and bullets is the inclusion of ordering in a numbered list. The numbering options available include letters, numerals, and Roman numerals (a system that uses specific letters to represent numeric values such as *I* for one and *V* for five).

FIGURE 3.24 Bullet Library in PowerPoint

3.3.3 Document Review

One of the biggest mistakes you can make with a presentation, or any other professional document, is not checking the spelling and grammar of the work before you submit it. PowerPoint has an excellent tool for checking spelling, but there are errors that it will not catch; for instance, typing the word "an" when you mean to type "and" may not register as a grammatical error and will not be flagged as a spelling error as it is a correctly spelled word. Because of this, it is a good idea to have someone else review your work before you present.

In addition to the manual tools for checking spelling and grammar, PowerPoint has several AutoCorrect features that will attempt to replace words as you type to correct common misspellings and to replace certain text entries with symbols.

You can configure the AutoCorrect options if you want to add any additional rules or turn off any existing rules. To reach the AutoCorrect preferences in PowerPoint 2013, select the *File* menu and then choose *Options*. This will open the *PowerPoint Options* dialog box. From here, click *Proofing* in the menu on the left and select the *AutoCorrect Options* button. In PowerPoint 2011, select the *Tools* menu and *AutoCorrect*. The existing rules are displayed in a list at the bottom of the dialog box; you can add a rule by typing the misspelled word in the *Replace* field followed by the correct word in the *With* field and choosing *Add*.

3.3.4 Find and Replace

An additional tool that can help you with searching for repetitive terms or finding a particular word in your presentation is the *Find* command. This allows you to perform a simple keyword search of your presentation. In PowerPoint 2013, the *Find* icon is located on the *Home* ribbon; you can also access the *Find* command on a Windows machine using the shortcut Ctrl-F. In PowerPoint 2011, there is an existing search box in the top-right corner of the open presentation window that will allow you to enter text for a keyword search of your presentation; you can highlight this search box using the shortcut *Command-F*. This will highlight all instances of the keyword (or words) in your presentation.

> **NOTE** *The keyword entry for the Find command in PowerPoint 2013 is located on the Navigation pane. If the Navigation pane is closed when you select the Find command (by icon or by using the shortcut, the Navigation pane will be displayed on the Browse Results tab. This tab will show all instances of the keyword in the presentation, and you can jump to a particular location by clicking on a result.*

To replace the keyword with which you searched the presentation with another term, you use the *Replace* command. In PowerPoint 2013, this is located on the *Home* ribbon; when activated, it will open a *Find and Replace* dialog box where you can navigate instance by instance through the presentation (with the *Find Next* button) or simply replace

FIGURE 3.25 Find and Replace dialog box in PowerPoint 2013

every instance of the keyword with the text you enter in the Replace field. The *Find and Replace* dialog box is shown in Figure 3.25. In PowerPoint 2013, you can activate the *Replace* command using the shortcut *Ctrl-H*. To open this same dialog box in PowerPoint 2011, select the *Edit* menu, select *Find*, and then choose *Advanced Find and Replace*.

3.3.5 Using Document Templates

A *template* is a preformatted placeholder presentation for your content; you can build your own instance of the presentation using the predefined areas where you can add objects and text, knowing what it will look like when you are finished. It is possible to modify templates just like any other presentation (you can even create custom templates), but templates save you work in formatting the presentation yourself or formatting the same presentation again. Document templates are a great way to get started with formatting if you are unsure of what your presentation should look like.

In PowerPoint 2013, you can create a new presentation from a template by selecting the *File* menu and choosing *New*. Beneath the blank

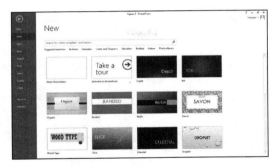

FIGURE 3.26 Template selection in PowerPoint 2013

presentation that you can select are the template selections. You can see an example of this in Figure 3.26.

In PowerPoint 2011, you can create a new presentation from a template either by selecting the *File* menu and choosing *New from Template* or by clicking the New from Template icon in the Quick Access toolbar. This will open the PowerPoint Document Gallery. You can select whichever template you want to use.

Regardless of the version you are using, your new presentation will open in a new window of PowerPoint.

ACTIVITY 3.4—USING THE ONEDRIVE TO STORE DOCUMENTS

For this activity, you will add your resume and cover letter to your OneDrive account. Use a Web browser of your choice and login to your Windows Live account. Select the OneDrive and choose the Upload option. Select both files to upload to your account. You should not set sharing on these files at this time. Where do these files appear on the main page of your OneDrive account online? What options are you given when you select one of them?

CHAPTER SUMMARY

This chapter introduced you to the fundamental concepts and operations for creating simple presentations. This is a common way to share information in businesses and organizations. In addition, this chapter covered the use of common File menu commands for most software applications, keyboard productivity shortcuts, and file and file type management. The next chapter expands on the use of presentation software to create more advanced presentations and give you exposure to the more complex formatting available in presentation creation. The menus and tasks introduced in this chapter will carry forward into other productivity tools you may encounter.

CHAPTER KNOWLEDGE CHECK

1. All of the following are operations that can typically be performed from the File menu in an application except:
   a. Opening a file
   b. Creating a new file
   c. Undoing the last command
   d. Saving a file

2. The following are valid formatting shortcuts for a Windows machine except:
   a. Ctrl-B
   b. Ctrl-I
   c. Ctrl-S
   d. Ctrl-U
   e. All of the above
   f. None of the above

3. The following operation is used to create a duplicate of selected text or objects on the system clipboard and remove the original:
   a. Copy
   b. Paste
   c. Format Painter
   d. Cut

4. Automated spelling and grammar checks will catch every spelling mistake possible in the language that is selected.
   a. True
   b. False

5. The following is not a characteristic of a bulleted list:
   a. You can select different symbols to display as the bullet point.
   b. The order of the items in the list is significant.
   c. You can have multiple levels of bullet points in an outline format.
   d. All of the above
   e. None of the above

PRACTICE EXERCISES

1. Begin by thinking about a hobby you enjoy where construction of some sort is involved. Using the Web, find additional research supporting facts about your hobby and then prepare a 5-slide presentation describing some aspect of your hobby. For example, you might like building model cars or assembling gift baskets. If you are not able to think of a personal hobby, then use the Web to develop step-by-step instructions on building or installing an object of your choice.

2. Using the Web, research a current legal issue affecting your community. For example, you might research a new law that is difficult to understand. Use your research to develop a 5-slide presentation to clarify what the law means.

3. Using presentation software, develop an outline that explains the steps used to cite sources in the writing style of your choice. Examples of these styles include APA and MLA format.

4. Create a presentation using every available slide layout. Compare the layout options and, for each layout, identify an ideal situation in which they would convey information in the best way. Use the presentation to construct these examples (the data included can be fictitious as long as the layout and form are correct).

CHAPTER 4

DEVELOPING MEDIA ENHANCED PRESENTATIONS

In This Chapter

This chapter is an introduction to the process for adding media and effects to your presentation. You will create a presentation and add images, clip art, hyperlinks, and screen captures. You will also explore the different text effects and shape formatting tools available to add style to your presentations. Once you have completed the chapter, you will be able to:

- Insert and format images and screenshots in a presentation document
- Insert drawing shapes and clip art into a presentation document
- Rearrange slides in a presentation document
- Add slide transitions to a presentation document

4.1 CREATING A MEDIA RICH PRESENTATION

For your first real foray into the media aspects of PowerPoint, you will construct a presentation on a very familiar subject: you! Create a new presentation and save it as *MyPowerPoint*. On the first slide, the *title slide*, you will see two *placeholder text boxes*. These text boxes contain text such as "Click to add ..." that will disappear the instant you start typing in one of them. You should be somewhat familiar with these at this point. An example of the title slide is shown in Figure 4.1. This is also a good time to practice applying themes. Apply the theme of your choice and type your name in the title placeholder.

ACTIVITY 4.1—PRACTICING THEMES

Create a new presentation and save it as *Activity4_1*. Next, you will apply a theme to your presentation. You can choose from any of the preset options.

Now, alter the theme using the available tools. You can adjust colors and fonts as well as the background. Be sure to remember the process you used because this will be a common activity when you are creating presentations. The theme options available may differ depending upon the version of PowerPoint you are using.

FIGURE 4.1 Example title slide

If you have a long name, it may split into two lines. To keep your first name and last name on the same line, you can widen the placeholder box by clicking on one of the square selection points around the perimeter of the text box, as shown in Figure 4.2. The left square selection

FIGURE 4.2 Selection points on a text box

point will only move the left edge of the box, and the right square selection point will only move the right edge of the box. Picking one of the round corner selection points lets you change both the width and height at the same time.

Switch the text alignment to the left by selecting the *Align Text Left* icon (or by pressing *Ctrl-L*) or to the right by selecting the *Align Text Right* icon (*Ctrl-R*). This is helpful to remember when you need to line up headings and text with one edge or the other. Titles, however, look better centered, so put your name back where it was by clicking the *Align Text Center* icon (*Ctrl-E*).

NOTE *If you are using a Mac, the Control (Ctrl) key shortcuts all work the same way, but they use the Command (or Apple) key instead of the Control key.*

4.1.1 Text Effects

Now your name is starting to show some pizzazz, but you should give it more flair by adding text effects. The various text effects are in the *Format* ribbon for *Drawing Tools*, which is context sensitive and appears whenever you click in a text box. Text effects are another type of formatting that adds elements like shadow, glow, reflection, and outlines to the letters in the text box. To apply an effect, you must select the text to which you want the effect to apply. To apply the effect to all of the text in the box, you can select the box surrounding the text. Some text effects, like 3-D Rotation and Transform, apply to the entire content of the text box and cannot be applied to individual letters or words.

NOTE *PowerPoint 2011 places a* Text Effects *icon on the lower-right corner of the* Font *panel of the* Home *ribbon.*

You can select a predefined overall style from the *Word Art Styles* panel of the context-sensitive *Format* ribbon or you can change elements individually. Too many text effects at once can ruin the appeal of your display. To test these on plain text, select *Text Effects*, then *Reflection*, and choose a reflection variation you like. Keep the reflection effect for this project, but to cancel it, select the *No Reflection* option in the drop-down menu. You can also fine-tune the reflection by selecting *Reflection Options* just as you did for the shadow effect.

ACTIVITY 4.2—TEXT EFFECTS

Using the presentation you are constructing for the lesson project, save a copy of it as *Activity4_2*. Give your name depth by adding a shadow. To do so, click the *Text Effects* icon, select *Shadow* from the drop-down list, and then select the one you want. You can also set the perspective of the shadow (the angle of the implied light source) by selecting one of the options at the end of the drop-down menu. Clicking *Shadow Options* will allow you to fine-tune the parameters to get your shadow effect just right. The *Distance* parameter, for example, will determine how far away the shadow is from your object. Now cancel the shadow by selecting *Text Effects*, then *Shadow*, and *No Shadow*. Save your work and test these steps on other text effects to see how they vary and what stays the same.

Click on the *subtitle* placeholder. Rather than enter text here, click on the outer perimeter of the subtitle placeholder box and get rid of it by pressing the *Delete* key or the *Backspace* key. You can do this to remove any placeholders that you do not want or to remove any objects you have added that you no longer like. You should now see a slide similar to Figure 4.3 except with your name in the box and the background style that you chose earlier.

4.1.2 Inserting and Formatting Shapes

Now you are going to show everyone what a superstar you are. If you are using PowerPoint 2013, switch over to the *Insert* ribbon and select the *Shapes* icon; if you are using PowerPoint 2011, the *Shape* icon is on the *Home* ribbon. Pick a star from the drop-down list and click inside the slide. This should stamp an instance of the shape wherever you click.

You can format the star by using the right-click menu or the familiar *Format* ribbon that appears whenever you click on a shape. This time it will be the *Shape Styles* panel in which you will find what you need. With the shape selected,

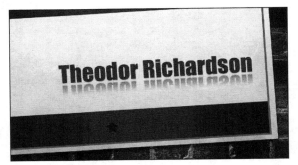

FIGURE 4.3 Completed example

right-clicking and selecting *Format Shape* will open a dialog box that lets you alter the properties of your star (this is the same dialog box that you get by selecting the expansion icon on the *Shape Styles* panel in PowerPoint 2013). The *Format Shape* dialog box is shown in Figure 4.4. Note that it appears as a dialog box in PowerPoint 2011 and as a new pane in PowerPoint 2013.

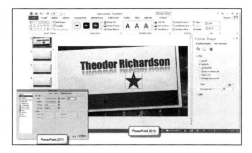

FIGURE 4.4 Format Shape dialog box for line settings

First, change the star's outline to something thick. Select *Line Style* in PowerPoint 2013; select *Line*, then *Weights & Arrows*, then *Style* in PowerPoint 2011. Increase the *Width* to *3 pt*. This should make the outline nice and bold. The *Dash Type* (or *Dashed*) setting determines how the line appears, whether you want a solid line or a dotted line that implies the shape.

In PowerPoint 2013, click on the *Line Color* item in the menu. You have a choice of No Line, Solid Line, or Gradient Line. Having no line would defeat the purpose of making it thicker, so opt for *Solid Line*. In PowerPoint 2011, select either the *Solid* or *Gradient* tab of the *Line* menu to change these settings; select *Solid,* and you should see the *Color* setting. Next, you need to choose a color that will work with your background but make the star stand out all the same; choose whatever color you like.

On the *Fill* menu, shown in Figure 4.5, you are going to make your star stand out by selecting a *Gradient* option. This menu will allow you to select from a set number of different gradients; if you are using PowerPoint 2013, you can pick one of the predefined gradients from the Preset Colors list.

You can set Type to *Linear* if you want the gradient to go from left to right or top to bottom or to *Radial* if you want it to start in the

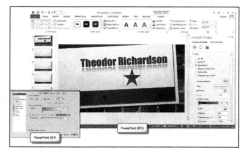

FIGURE 4.5 Format Shape dialog box for gradient fill settings

center and work its way around a curve. The stops of the gradient are shown on the bar beneath these settings. You can add or delete stops, but the program will interpolate the color from one stop to the next. Click on any of the stops to change the color yourself. The Rotate with shape option determines whether the gradient is created based on the orientation of the slide or the orientation of the shape itself.

NOTE
Shortcuts to the Line *and* Fill *menu options are available on the* Format *ribbon.*

When you are done setting the color, click *Close* (or *OK*) to exit the dialog box in PowerPoint 2011 or click the *X* at the right of the pane in PowerPoint 2013. You can now resize the star based on just how big of a superstar you are. Use either the round corner grab points or the square midpoint grab points to change the size of the shape. The circle at the top of the shape (which looks like an arrow turning in PowerPoint 2013) can be used to rotate the shape. Simply click and hold the circle and give your shape a spin. You may see one or more small yellow diamonds or circle inside your shape. These control internal parameters of the shape; for instance, this will set how fat or skinny the triangular legs of your star become.

Finally, make that star shine. Click on the star and select the *Format* ribbon. Click the *Shape Effects* icon, select *Glow*, and pick a glow that fits your star. You can also set the color of the glow by selecting *More Glow Colors* (or *Glow Options* in PowerPoint 2011) from the menu. This will open a color picker from which you can choose the color you want your star to shine. When you are done, you should have a shining star beneath your name as in Figure 4.6.

FIGURE 4.6 Completed example

Now you need to add the "Super" to your star. To do this in PowerPoint 2013, select the *Insert* ribbon and pick the *WordArt* icon; in PowerPoint 2011, select *WordArt* from the drop-down list under *Text* on the *Home* ribbon. This works similarly to using the predefined styles for text formatting on the *Format* ribbon. In PowerPoint 2013, choose a style from the menu that appears.

This action will create a text box in your slide. Change the text inside to *Super* and position it where you want it on the slide. This works just like any other text box with some of the settings completed for you. You can still change the font and the size, along with any other properties.

Click on your new text box and go to the *Format* ribbon that appears. Select the *Text Effects* icon and then select *Transform*. Pick a transformation for your text. Now go back to the *Home* ribbon and change the font color or the font. The transformation and overall formatting that was defined should remain intact. Small pink diamonds in your text box will control properties like the angle of the text slant when you click on them and slide them in one direction or another.

Maybe you are more of a rockstar than a superstar. It is easy enough to change the text to represent that. Just double-click the text box to select it and all of its contents. Now type *Rock* in the box. There you go! Now you have instant "Rockstar" status, and you are just getting started! Compare your rockstar results to Figure 4.7, which shows the elements you should have when you are finished.

FIGURE 4.7 Completed example

4.1.3 Inserting, Manipulating, and Cropping Images

It is time to show your smiling face to the world. Go to the second slide in your presentation. If you have not added a second slide yet, simply right-click in the *Slides/Outline* pane and select *New Slide*. This second slide should have the default layout for a slide, which consists of a slide title placeholder text box and a single box for content, as shown in Figure 4.8. You are going to add a picture here, so you may want to pick a nice image of yourself. For those of you who are camera shy, you can use an image of a monkey making a silly face instead.

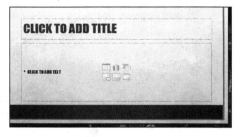

FIGURE 4.8 New slide with the default layout

Before you start typing in the content box, which will eliminate the quick links, select the *Insert Picture from File* icon on the slide. This is the same as selecting *Picture* on the *Insert* ribbon (*Picture* is on the *Home* ribbon in PowerPoint 2011); it just saves you a few clicks of the mouse. Using the quick link allows you to select the image and then insert and center it under the title of the slide. Notice that this will replace the placeholder text box entirely. Go ahead and give your slide a title and make sure it is appropriate for what the slide contains. Quickly practice your text modification techniques and create a style to make your title stand out from the background.

Now click back on the image you just inserted. You will see a new ribbon along the top of the interface. This is the *Format ribbon for Picture Tools* (the *Format Picture* ribbon in PowerPoint 2011). As you can see from Figure 4.9, this ribbon contains a lot of tools for making your picture look superb.

On the *Picture Styles* panel, select one of the predefined styles that will make the image look like an old printout from a handheld instant camera. Something with a nice thick white border will be perfect. On the *Adjust* panel, select the *Corrections* icon; this allows you to increase or decrease the

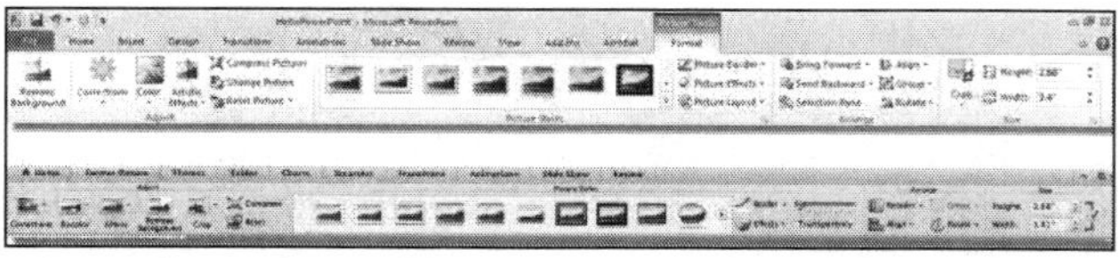

FIGURE 4.9 Format ribbon for Picture Tools in PowerPoint 2013 and Format Picture ribbon in PowerPoint 2011

brightness, contrast, and sharpness of the image. The original image will appear in the center of the options, and you can adjust it by clicking one of the options around it. Increase the contrast slightly to give your photo a richer tone.

There are a number of settings that can be used to correct a picture that is inserted into PowerPoint. There is a preview visualization of the effect whenever a transformation is selected, but the following list will help you understand these transformation terms:

- Color Saturation—*This is the term for how pure the color is; the higher the saturation, the purer the color. The primary colors red, blue, and green are the purest (and most saturated) colors.*
- Color Tone—*The color tone is how light or dark the color is. Each color can produce a spectrum of tones. The tone value is relative, so the surrounding colors will affect the perception of the tone.*
- Sharpen and Soften—*This setting will vary how clear the differentiation is between neighboring pixels of the image. Sharpen will increase the differentiation by more strongly defining boundaries in the image. Soften will decrease the differentiation by blending together the colors of the image.*
- Brightness and Contrast—*Brightness is the threshold for the color level that registers as black; higher brightness means there are more colors allowed between pure white and pure black. Contrast is a measure of the spectrum of colors between pure white and pure black; higher contrast will generally show more granular detail of the image.*

Now turn your photo to grayscale. You can do this by selecting the *Color* icon in the *Adjust* panel (this is called *Recolor* in PowerPoint 2011). This gives you options to select the color saturation, color tone, and recolor options. Under *Recolor*, select *Grayscale*. The *Adjust* panel has some other useful items as well. Along the right side of the *Adjust* panel are the following options:

- *Compress Picture* will reduce the file size of the PowerPoint file by sampling the picture to the necessary resolution for the screen.
- *Reset Picture* will undo all of the formatting you added since inserting the image at the beginning.

The next thing you need to do is crop the image so that it focuses better on the subject. Cropping allows you to remove parts from the top, bottom, left, or right of the image that you do not want to display. Click on the image and then select *Crop* on the *(Picture) Format* ribbon. Now you can use any of the grab points on the image and move them in toward the center to cut off portions of the image you do not want instead of just resizing the image in place. This process is shown in Figure 4.10.

FIGURE 4.10 Cropping an image

Cropping is the act of cutting off outer portions of an image or object. This is the digital equivalent of using scissors to cut off pieces of an image on paper.

The *Crop* icon has some other useful options. For instance, you can crop your image to a drawing shape. Selecting any of these options will override your manual cropping. There are two more predefined options that you may find useful:

- *Crop to Fill* causes the entire image to be forced to the area defined by cropping. This will fill the cropped space with as much of the image as possible, cutting off only what is necessary to preserve the defined space.
- *Crop to Fit* causes the image to be forced in its entirety to the defined space. This may cause gaps in the display if no image information is available to match the space defined.

You can click and drag the image you have inserted to resize it just like any other drawing or graphic object inserted into your slides. The one thing you must remember with pictures is that you should always maintain the original aspect ratio of the image. Otherwise, faces and bodies will look stretched or pinched when you distort the image. This not only looks bad, but it will also grab the attention of your audience in a negative way because their eyes will be drawn to the distortion instead of what you want them to see.

> *Aspect ratio* is the longer dimension of an object divided by the shorter dimension. This is the ratio that should be preserved whenever any changes are made to an object to avoid distortion. The aspect ratio of a standard 5 x 3 photograph is 5:3.

4.1.4 Arranging, Linking, and Grouping Elements

The old saying is that a picture is worth a thousand words. Well, you are going to add a few more for your picture. Before you get to that, though, you need to move the image back into alignment after it has been cropped. The image was originally centered in the placeholder, but the changes made to it have altered its position on the slide.

> *Alignment* in terms of layout is the relative placement of an object with respect to the overall environment, which in this case is the slide.

The alignment commands are under the *Arrange* icon in the *Home* ribbon. Click on *Arrange* and scroll down to *Align*; you should see all of the options for orienting your picture around the screen. The full path is shown in Figure 4.11. These alignment commands work on any element you insert into your presentation. You can also find a shortcut to the alignment options (as an *Align* icon) on the context-sensitive *Format* ribbons that appear.

Make sure the *Align to Slide* box has a check mark beside it. This will make all of your alignment adjustments relative to the slide itself. If this is not checked,

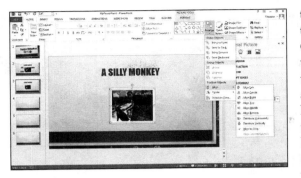

the elements will align relative to each other. Click the *Align Center* item in the menu to line up your photo to the center of the slide. Click on the photo and press the up or down arrow keys to move it to the center of the lower portion of the slide beneath the title. You can hold down the *Control* (Ctrl) key on your keyboard and press the arrows to move it a smaller distance for each arrow press.

FIGURE 4.11 Menu path to alignment options

Now you are going to revisit the *Shapes* icon and select a rectangle. You can just pick one and click in your slide to stamp it down, or you can make your selection and click and drag on the slide to set the size yourself. Click on your new rectangle and copy it. You can do this by right-clicking on the object and selecting *Copy* or you can press *Ctrl-C* on the keyboard with the object selected. Now paste two more rectangles into your slide.

In PowerPoint 2013, you can do this by right-clicking where you want the rectangle to appear and selecting *Picture* under the *Paste Options*. You can also do this by pressing *Ctrl-V* on the keyboard, which will give you the default paste settings. In PowerPoint 2011, selecting *Paste* from the right-click menu or pressing the shortcut keys to paste will result in a copy placed on top of the original but slightly to the right and down.

Click on one of the rectangles and start typing. Type a descriptive word for the image, such as *Charming*, and notice how the shape automatically accepts the text. Now add two more descriptive words to the other rectangles; you could try *Witty* and *Slobbery*, for instance. Almost all of the drawing shapes allow you to directly insert text into them; the area of the shape allocated for text will vary, so the length of text may be limited depending on the shape you choose. You can format these shapes just as you did the star in the previous example, and you can format the text inside the shapes as well.

There is a special kind of shape that can connect two elements in your slide. These are found under the *Line* (or *Lines and Connectors*) heading in the *Shapes* menu. Click on an arrow that you like and your cursor will change to a crosshair. Whenever you roll your mouse over an element, you will see small red squares appear; these are linking points for the shape. You can connect a line from one of these linking points to another or draw a line without linking it. For this example, you will place one end of the line on the rectangles containing the descriptive words and link the other end to the picture.

NOTE *In PowerPoint 2013, you can hold down the Alt key to allow you to freely move the line's endpoint when you are dragging an arrow; otherwise, the endpoint will align to the closest internal grid point available.*

If you connect an endpoint of your line to an element, the line will stay connected even if that element is moved. An unconnected end will not stay where it is placed when an object to which it is connected is moved; it will move around with the rest of the object to which it is connected. If neither end is connected, the object will have to be moved manually just like any other object.

FIGURE 4.12 Arrow settings

To format the ends of your arrows and change how they are displayed, you can use both the usual tools for formatting and the *Format Shape* dialog box, which contains the arrow settings in the panel under *Line Styles* (you need to select *Line* and then *Weights & Arrows* in PowerPoint 2011). Here you can change the Begin Type (Begin Style) or End Type (End Style) for the arrow (which affects either the initial or final point of the arrow, respectively) and set the size you want for each; this is shown in Figure 4.12.

Link the rest of your rectangles to your photo with arrows. Format the arrows so they are clearly visible on the slide. You may notice that the arrows you place are on top of the rectangles; this is because any new element added to your slide automatically gets placed in the highest layer available. You will want to put your rectangles on top of the arrows to make the slide look more presentable. To do this, you will need to change the layer on which these elements reside. Think of these items like sheets of paper in a stack. To move an element to the top of the stack, you need to bring it forward. To move it to the bottom of the stack, you need to send it back. You can think of the slide background as the table on which this stack is sitting; nothing can be sent behind the slide itself.

There are two ways to change the layer of an element. You can right-click the element and choose either *Bring to Front* or *Send to Back* (to put it on the very top or bottom, respectively) or use *Bring Forward* or *Send Backward* to change the layer by one position at a time. You can also select the element and click the *Arrange* icon. In PowerPoint 2013, *Order Objects* is the first heading you will see on this menu, and it contains all of your options for adjusting the layer. Select each rectangle and choose *Bring to Front*.

PowerPoint 2011 has a great feature to visualize the layers on the slide and allow you to rearrange them. Under the Arrange icon, you can select Reorder Objects or Reorder Overlapping Objects. This

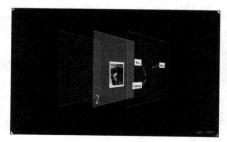

FIGURE 4.13 Visualizing layers in PowerPoint 2011

NOTE *launches a visual display of the layers in your slide that you can click and drag to reorder as shown in Figure 4.13. This is also a great visualization of the layers to determine what is visible to the viewer.*

FIGURE 4.14 Completed example with grouping

Now that you have a nice arrangement for your elements (you should have all of the same elements as in Figure 4.14), you do not want anyone to accidentally move something around if they edit your presentation. A good solution to this is to create a *group* for these objects so they all act like a single element in the slide.

To create a group, click outside of the group and hold down the mouse button while you drag your cursor over all of the items you want to group. Then you can either right-click within the group and select *Group* or you can go to the *Home* ribbon, select the *Arrange* icon, and select *Group*. You can also hold down the *Shift* key while clicking on each object you want to group and then follow the steps to create the group.

NOTE *Note that if an object is inserted into a placeholder, it cannot be included in a group. To get around this, copy the element, paste the copy, and delete the original and the placeholder. The copy can then be included in the group.*

You can still select individual objects from the group by clicking on any one of them (as in Figure 4.14). If you decide these objects need to be separated, click on the whole group, right-click, and select *Ungroup* (this is also available as an option under the *Arrange* icon on the *Home* ribbon). If they need to be put back together, select *Regroup* and the old group will be back together again.

4.1.5 Adding Text and Hyperlinks

Now it is time to start adding text to the PowerPoint presentation. Before you use PowerPoint to write that novel you have been planning, there are some things you should know about what PowerPoint should and should not be. First of all, there are two main reasons to construct a PowerPoint document: to create a visual supplement to a presentation and to create a small multimedia presentation for sharing on a computer. PowerPoint text should be brief and easy to read, no matter what purpose the presentation has. You should always keep your bullet points short and meaningful. Presentation software is excellent at showcasing information when it is used in this manner. If you are giving your PowerPoint presentation to an audience, you have to keep readability in mind. Small fonts and changing styles on the same slide are difficult to read.

Add a third slide for your presentation about yourself. Here you are going to explore some of the tools for adding and modifying text in a PowerPoint slide. You can choose here whether you want to include a list of foods you like to eat or a list of hobbies you enjoy; both of these would help describe you and are a good fit for a casual presentation like this. Whichever you choose, go

FIGURE 4.15 Bulleted list in the default slide arrangement

ahead and type a title for your slide. Practice your formatting skills by making sure it matches the appearance of the title text on the slide with your photo on it.

Now choose four or five items to support your title. The example in Figure 4.15 shows five things to eat that begin with the letter *P*. Click in the placeholder text box of the slide (with a default layout) and type your items in a similar manner. You should notice that these are formatted as a list; this is the default format and it makes it easy to distinguish your points as you have seen already. In a presentation, the text does not have to be in complete sentences; the essential thing is to get your points across in as clear and concise a manner as possible.

You should also notice how you have a lot of space left over on this slide. You can either add subtext to each bullet or increase the font size to take up more space. If this is being used for a visual presentation on a projector or screen behind you, make sure you change the font to a sans serif font (such as Arial or Calibri). All those text decorations (the serifs) make the text more difficult to read on a projection. If the presentation is being shared by computer, serif fonts are fine because it is closer to print media format.

Expand your list a little bit by choosing a topic for which you want to add subtext. Note that you should only add subtext if you have at least two things to say about a topic. A single element of subtext looks messy and unorganized; it is also a violation of the rules of outlining. Click on the line for which you want to add text; place your cursor at the end of the text and hit the *Enter* key.

You should see a new line beneath your text with a new bullet beside it that looks grayed out as if it is not completely there. If you start typing now, you will enter text at the same level (level 1) as the original item, so press the *Tab* key to turn this line into subtext for the line above it. Now you should see the bullet type change and the text cursor indent farther into the page to the right. Your text will now be

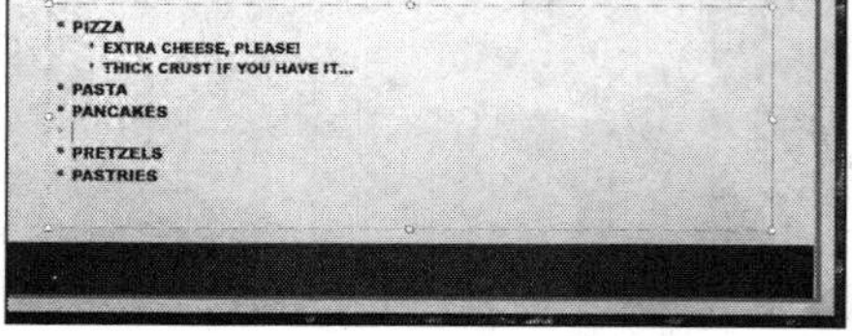

FIGURE 4.16 Two-level bullet list

smaller and it will be formatted as the next level down (level 2) in terms of your outline. You can see this in action in Figure 4.16.

You can modify your text using the *Paragraph* panel of the *Home* ribbon. This is where you can change the bullet styles for your slide or even change them to numbers if you need your list to be in a specific order. Unless you make the change in the *Slide Master*, this only changes the bullet style for the current slide in which you are working and only for the bullet points that you have highlighted when you click the icon.

NOTE
In PowerPoint 2013, if you type too much text for one slide, a little box will pop up to give you options on what to do. You can choose to change your slide layout or split the content of the text box between two slides. You should always take note when this box appears because it means your slide is starting to get too crowded.

You can set a number of other useful properties with the *Paragraph* panel, including changing the direction of your text, the number of columns, or the text alignment inside the text box. You can adjust the line spacing and indentation of the text as well.

Now create a new slide (this should be the fourth slide of your presentation); this is where you are going to add some contact information so all of your fans can reach you once they see how great you are. For the title of the slide, add the text *How to Reach Me* and make sure you format it to match the titles of the rest of your slides. This is good practice and it keeps your slides from looking out of place when you click from one to the next.

Consider carefully what you want to add to this page. You probably do not want to give out your home address or personal phone number on a slide that can be seen by anyone. If you have a Facebook page or an email address that you don't mind being seen (and used) by the public, you can add those here. When you type any text into PowerPoint that matches the format for a Website or email address, PowerPoint will automatically convert the text into a hyperlink. Just like a hyperlink on the Web, when you click on this text, it will either take you to the location specified or open your email account so you can send a message to this address.

Unless you have multiple links or addresses, you probably do not need a bullet point for this slide. To get rid of bullet points on this or any slide, just click at the beginning of the text and press the *Backspace* key (or the *Delete* key for PowerPoint 2011). The bullet point will disappear and your text will no longer be in outline format. With just one item on the page, there is a lot of empty space that can make your slide look bad, even if you increase the font size dramatically.

To correct this, move your link to the horizontal center of the slide by selecting the *Center* icon to center the text (which you can find under the *Paragraph* panel of the *Home* ribbon). You can also move your text to the vertical center of the text box by selecting the *Middle* item in the *Align Text* menu that opens; this icon is in the same panel as the horizontal text alignment options. Your text should now be centered within the text box; note that this does not center it on the slide or center the text box itself.

Now you can use the font tools to increase the size of the link so it takes up more space. Remember that readability is crucial for a presentation, so you may want to stretch your text box so you can increase the size of the hyperlink beyond the original box size to make it easier to see. If you change the width of the text box, make sure you use the selections in the *Arrange* icon to align it back to the horizontal center of your slide. You can change the font, text effects, and style just like you would any other text in your presentation. The exception to this is the color of the hyperlink text.

To give the color of the link a higher level of contrast to the background, you must set the Hyperlink color in the theme color settings. In PowerPoint 2013, you access this setting in the *Design* ribbon by selecting the drop-down icon of the *Variants* panel and selecting *Colors* and then *Customize*

FIGURE 4.17 Create New Theme Colors dialog box in PowerPoint 2013

Colors. In PowerPoint 2011, you access this setting by selecting the *Themes* ribbon, selecting *Colors*, and then selecting *Create Theme Colors*. A dialog box like the one in Figure 4.17 will open and you can select the color you want for your link by using the color picker for *Hyperlink*.

Once you click *Save* (or *Apply to All* in PowerPoint 2011) in this dialog box, all of the hyperlinks in your presentation will be updated to the new color. PowerPoint treats your hyperlink colors as all or nothing, so you should be sure that the color you choose works on all of your slides. Note that you can give a name to your custom color scheme in this dialog box as well if you want to use it later. If you do not, it will still appear with the default name *Custom1* in this presentation because it is now in use.

If you want your text to display something other than an email address or the URL to which you are linking, you can use the *Hyperlink* icon. In PowerPoint 2013, you will find this under the *Links* panel of the *Insert* ribbon; in PowerPoint 2011, you will find the *Hyperlink* icon as an entry in the *Text* icon menu on the *Home* ribbon. Clicking this icon will open a dialog box in which you can select another document, enter a URL for a Website, or enter an email address. You can change the text that will be visible on the document for the link in the *Text to display* (or *Display*) box. You can also click on the *ScreenTip* button to enter text that will appear if the mouse hovers over the link. If you are not using the address of the link itself, you may want to add the address to the ScreenTip text so a user will know where they are headed when they click the hyperlink. The ScreenTip will only display in the Slide Show view,

FIGURE 4.18 ScreenTip in Slide Show view

as shown in Figure 4.18. It will not appear in the *Normal* view as you are editing the document.

If you add a hyperlink that you later decide you do not want, you can select any part of the text that contains the hyperlink, right-click, and select *Remove Hyperlink* in PowerPoint 2013 or you can click on the *Hyperlink* icon and click *Remove Link* on the open *Edit Hyperlink* dialog box. In PowerPoint 2011, right-click the link, select *Hyperlink*, then *Edit Hyperlink*, and then click *Remove Hyperlink* on the dialog box that opens. Another way to remove the link in either version is to place your cursor just past the last letter of the hyperlink. Click *Backspace* (or *Delete* in PowerPoint 2011) on the keyboard and you should see the underline disappear; now your link is gone.

NOTE *If you have typed a URL or email address, pressing the spacebar after the address will create an automatic link, no matter how many times you have removed it!*

4.1.6 Adding Actions

Now you will practice adding actions to an item in your presentation. These actions can be applied to images and media elements and will cause a behavior that you set as a response to the item being clicked in *Slide Show* view. To practice this, you will add a behavior to the image you added to your slides.

Adding an action to an object in your presentation allows you to do all sorts of advanced things on your PowerPoint slides. In PowerPoint 2013, you can find the *Action* icon on the *Insert* ribbon. In PowerPoint 2011, *Action Settings* is part of the right-click menu; it can also be found as an icon on the *Slide Show* ribbon. It is not the best tool to use if you are giving a linear presentation to an audience, but if you are sharing the presentation on a computer, this allows you to link up different slides and presentations and lets you run programs from within PowerPoint.

NOTE *Adding an action will automatically add a ScreenTip containing the address to which it is connected.*

For now, you are going to select the *Hyperlink to:* radio button and choose *URL*. This will prompt you for an address that you want to activate with the action. If you are using an email address, add *mailto:* before your address in the text box. For this example, you should use your public Facebook profile or just a Website that you like. You can see an example of these action settings in Figure 4.19.

You can edit this action at any time by selecting the image and using the *Action* (or *Action Settings*) icon that you used to start the process.

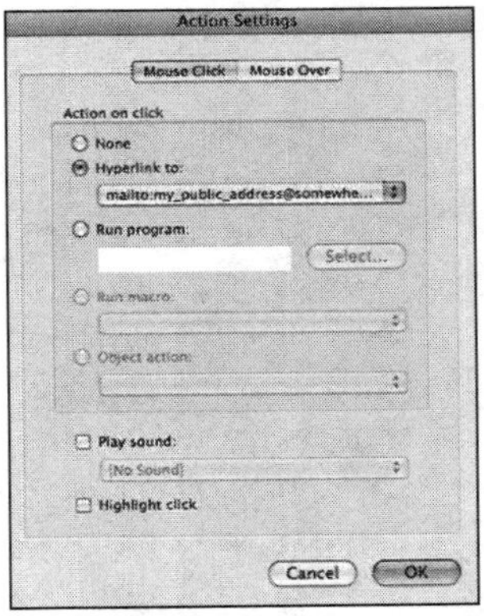

FIGURE 4.19 Example Action Settings dialog box

FIGURE 4.20 Example slide with action enabled image

Just like the hyperlink you added earlier, the action will not occur in *Normal* view. It will only work in the *Slide Show* view, which is shown in Figure 4.20. Actions are primarily used to open Web pages, move to other slides, or open documents or programs from within PowerPoint. This latter action is one of the reasons you should be sure you know the source before opening a PowerPoint file someone else has made.

4.1.7 Inserting Screenshots

Add a new slide with the default layout. Click in the title placeholder and type *This Is What My Work Looks Like* and format the text appropriately to match the rest of your slides. You may need to widen the placeholder to keep all of this text on a single line. Remember to align the placeholder to the center of the slide if you change its width so it is not off-center from the rest of your slide titles. Aligning the text box is separate from aligning the text. You are going to show everyone what your computer looks like when you are hard at work. Make sure you have a program open that you use frequently.

Now click the placeholder in the lower part of the slide. If you are using PowerPoint 2013, you can just go to the *Insert* ribbon and select *Screenshot* from the *Images* panel. This is an easy way to capture what is happening in a live application on your machine. The menu that appears will show each open application (other than PowerPoint) and allow you to insert an image capture of that program into your slide. You can also select the *Screen Clipping* option from this menu and select an area of the screen you want to copy into an image. This is an incredibly useful tool for describing and displaying applications or showing an example Website in a presentation without having to leave PowerPoint.

If you are using PowerPoint 2011, this option is not available to you, but you can create a screen capture by holding down *Shift+Command+3*. This will place an image of your current computer screen on your computer desktop. You will hear a camera clicking sound if you do this correctly. You can now insert this image into your presentation just as you would any other image stored on your computer. Holding down *Shift+Command+4* lets you select an area of the screen to capture using the mouse. If you hold down the *Control* key along with either sequence (such as *Control+Shift+Command+3*), you will copy the image to your system clipboard so you can paste it directly into your slides.

You can generally save a screenshot on a Windows machine using keyboard shortcuts. This is typically done by pressing the *Print Screen* button, typically abbreviated *Prt Scn* or *Prt Sc*. This procedure will vary from computer to computer based on the keyboard layout, so you may have to look up how to do this on your individual machine if you do not have a single button for this. This procedure will copy your current desktop image to the clipboard of the system as a graphic.

FIGURE 4.21 Completed example with inserted screenshot

> *Whenever you are using a screen capture tool, make sure you are not exposing private or confidential information from you or your organization. It is your responsibility to make sure whatever is included in that screenshot, regardless of its size or readability, is allowed to be used and shared publicly.*

NOTE

Once the screenshot is inserted, you can work with it just like any other image you have included in your slides. You can add effects to it or crop it to suit your needs. Just remember that it is likely that the content of the inserted image will be difficult for an audience to read, so once again you should be sure that the point you are trying to make is apparent and that you are not giving your audience an eye exam by forcing them to read text that is too small to see. An example of the completed slide can be seen in Figure 4.21.

4.2 CLIP ART

Because presentation software is a visual medium for expression, it makes sense to add some visual elements to your slides beyond just screen captures and photographs. The most common of these elements by far is clip art. Microsoft maintains an enormous repository of clip art images for you to use to enhance your documents. Select the slide with the list of items you created. If you have been following along, this should be Slide 3. You are going to add an element of clip art to this page to enhance your presentation. The handling of clip art is significantly different in PowerPoint 2013 and PowerPoint 2011, so separate sections have been provided to guide you on how to get the same results in either program.

4.2.1 Clip Art in Office 2013

Adding clip art is fully integrated into the PowerPoint 2013 and Word 2013 environments. Go to the *Images* panel in the *Insert* ribbon and select *Online Pictures*. A dialog box will open, allowing you to select the source of

FIGURE 4.22 Online picture selection in PowerPoint 2013

the media you want, as shown in Figure 4.22. This contains a search box for your selection. In this case, you will select *Office.com Clip Art*.

When you press enter, the search will begin and a new screen will appear to display the results of the search. You can select one or more items from the list that appears and then choose *Insert* to add them to your slide. You can see an example of this in Figure 4.23. If you select more than one item, you should take note that they will all be added to the active slide.

FIGURE 4.23 Office.com Clip Art search results in PowerPoint 2013

4.2.2 Clip Art in Office 2011

PowerPoint 2011 has two options for directly inserting clip art into your presentation. The first is called the Clip Art Browser (which is shown in Figure 4.24); you can access this by clicking on the *Picture* icon on the *Home* ribbon to open the menu where you can select *Clip Art Browser*. This will open a panel of locally stored and indexed clip art images. If you want to place one of these images in the slide, just click on the image and drag it to the slide. You will see a small green plus sign on the image when you are over an area where it can be placed.

The second option is to select *Clip Art* Gallery, which is also found on the menu under *Picture* in the *Home* ribbon. This option will launch a

FIGURE 4.24 Clip Art Browser in PowerPoint 2011

FIGURE 4.25 Microsoft Clip Art Gallery

standalone application called Microsoft Clip Gallery, shown in Figure 4.25. Here you can search for a specific item you want or select categories. You can also configure your clip art categories, image classifications, and image tags and add new media to your collection using the *Import* button. To add one of the clip art items to your slide, select the graphic you want and click the *Insert* button.

4.2.3 Getting Clip Art from Office.com

Whether you are using PowerPoint or alternative software, you can download clips from Office.com (*www.office.com*) to add to your presentation or document. Simply go to the Office.com site and select the *Images* tab. You will then be able to select a category and perform a search on existing clip art within the Office.com repository. If you do not find what you want in that category, you can use the navigation pane on the left side to change the category or find results from all categories. If you visit the site using Microsoft Internet Explorer, the ActiveX® tools allow you to copy the image directly from the site to your system clipboard, as shown in Figure 4.26. You can then simply use the Paste function (or *Ctrl+P*) to paste the item into your slides.

If you visit Office.com with an Internet browser other than Internet Explorer, you can still use the clip art that is offered, but you have to download it to a local folder on your machine to make use of it. You do this by clicking on the clip art graphic you want and selecting *Download*. You can add this image

FIGURE 4.26 Clip Art options from Office.com using Internet Explorer

into your clip art repository by importing it into your media manager for Office 2011 or using the *Insert* ribbon and choosing *Pictures* to browse to its location on your machine for PowerPoint 2013.

4.2.4 Handling Clip Art

Once you have inserted the clip art image you want into your slide, you can manipulate it just like any other image, including recoloring it, adding shadows and effects, or reorienting it to suit your needs. You can open the *Rotate* (or *Rotate and Flip*) menu item in the *Arrange* icon menu to select common adjustments like *Flip Horizontal*.

You should take note that visual elements added to your page will make it more visually interesting, but they will distract the viewer from the text itself. The eye will focus on the location with the most visual information, which will typically be the image; this means your audience will see a picture before they see the text that goes with it. Too much of a good thing can turn bad when it comes to clip art. Limit your slides to a single clip art image unless you have a specific point that you are making with the visual component.

ACTIVITY 4.3—USING CLIP ART

Save a copy of your example presentation for the chapter project as *Activity4_3*. You are going to add and format a clip art graphic for the slide containing the foods you like to eat. Select one of the terms and perform a search for clip art that represents this food. Be sure to note the categories and options you needed to use in order to find suitable results. Once the image is added to your slide, practice using the formatting tools to alter the color and image effects applied to the clip art image. Be sure to save your work.

4.3 SORTING SLIDES

It is often necessary to reorganize and resort your slides to make sure your information is in the proper sequence. PowerPoint allows you to change the slide order at any time when you are working on your presentation. You can do this in one of two ways:

- Click on the *Slide Sorter View* icon at the bottom of the interface. Once this view is open, all of your slides will display on a grid as shown in Figure 4.27. You can simply click and hold your mouse on the last slide and drag it to where you want it to appear (in this case, imme-

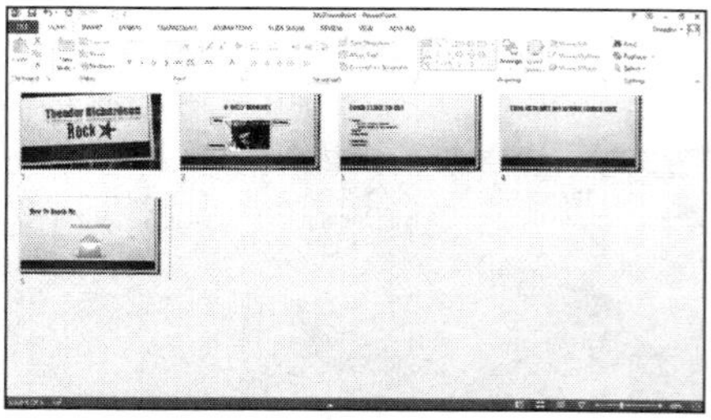

FIGURE 4.27 Slide Sorter view

diately before the contact slide). Click on the *Normal View* icon in the same location to get back to your slide design in *Normal* view. You can also double-click on a slide in the *Slide Sorter* view to open the *Normal* view on that particular slide.

- You can also reorder slides in the *Slides/Outline* pane on the left of the interface. To do this, just click and hold the slide you want to move and drag it to the position you want it to occupy.

4.4 TRANSITIONS

To complete your masterpiece, you should add transitions to your slides. By default, the slides will just change without any transition animation whatsoever. This may be suitable for a business presentation, but you may find instances in which you want a little style in your slide transitions. PowerPoint does not lack for transition options, which range from simple wipe effects to full-fledged animations of your slide being dissolved into a honeycomb and reassembled as the next slide. When adding transitions, make sure the animation does not overshadow the purpose of your presentation. Your audience did not come to see the animations you have constructed for your slide transitions.

With that said, you can use this presentation to experiment with elaborate transitions. You will find them all on the *Transitions* ribbon, shown in Figure 4.28. The Transition to This Slide panel has a selection of animations from which you can choose. The *Effect Options* icon will change depending on the transition that you select. For the introduction slide, something simple like a fade should be used. Click the *Apply to All* (or *Apply to All Slides* in PowerPoint 2011) icon on the *Transition* ribbon to apply the effect you have configured to every one of your slides. Once you have selected a transition for a slide, you will notice that a small icon appears next to your slide in the *Slides/Outline* pane on the left side of the interface. Click this icon to preview the attached animation.

The Duration setting determines how long the transition takes. If you are using your slide show as a visual supplement for a live presentation, you probably want short transitions, if you want any at all. You can also add sound to your transition by selecting one of the preset sound effects from the Sound menu. Sound that is used to excess is very annoying to an audience, and it can be very distracting if you have it playing over narration.

In this case, though, give yourself some applause on your introduction slide. You've earned it! To do this, select the drop-down list next to the word *Sound* and select *Applause*. Press *F5* to play your slide show in *Slide Show* view.

FIGURE 4.28 Transitions ribbon in PowerPoint 2013 and PowerPoint 2011

Take a bow because you have just completed your first media rich PowerPoint presentation!

ACTIVITY 4.4—TRANSITIONS

Save a copy of your example presentation for the chapter project as *Activity4_4*. Apply a different transition to each slide. Preview your transitions in Slide Show View. What options are available to adjust the length of each transition? What other customizations are possible for the transitions you chose? Be sure to save your work.

CHAPTER SUMMARY

This chapter provided an introduction to adding media into a presentation. This includes images, shapes, clip art, screenshots, hyperlinks, actions, and transitions. This chapter gave you an overview of the fundamental tools you need to build exciting and engaging presentations, but these are just the beginning when it comes to making your presentations work. The next chapter focuses on how to create and present your presentation effectively. You will get an idea of how to format your presentation to suit your purpose and audience, as well as gain an understanding of the most efficient and effective ways to showcase your ideas.

CHAPTER KNOWLEDGE CHECK

1. The Print Screen button on a PC, typically abbreviated *Prt Scn* or *Prt Scr*, can be used to copy your current desktop image to the clipboard of the system as a graphic.
    a. True
    b. False

2. Selecting the _____ in PowerPoint 2011 launches a visual display of the layers in your slide, which you can click and drag to reorder.
    a. Review ribbon
    b. Layer icon
    c. Animations ribbon
    d. Reorder Objects menu item

3. You can add a link to an email address or URL manually by selecting the _____.
    a. Format icon
    b. Hyperlink icon
    c. Color icon
    d. None of the above

4. The keyboard shortcut on a Windows PC that copies an object on the screen is _____, and _____can be used to paste the copied object.
    a.   *Ctrl-C, Ctrl-V*
    b.   *Ctrl-V, Ctrl-X*
    c.   *Ctrl-X, Ctrl-C*
    d.   Both a and b

5. Clip art can be retrieved and inserted into a presentation document using _____.
    a.   PowerPoint 2013
    b.   PowerPoint 2011
    c.   Office.com
    d.   All of the above
    e.   None of the above
    f.   Both a and b

PRACTICE EXERCISES

1. Begin by thinking about a hobby you enjoy where construction of some sort is involved. Using the Web, find additional research supporting facts about your hobby and then prepare a 10-slide presentation describing the steps you would take to build or assemble some aspect concerning your hobby. For example, you might like building model cars or assembling gift baskets. If you are not able to think of a personal hobby, then use the Web to develop step-by-step instructions on building or installing an object of your choice.

2. Using the Web, research a current legal issue affecting your community. For example, you might research a new law that is difficult to understand. Use your research to develop a 10-slide presentation to clarify what the law means. Make sure you add transitions, images, and hyperlinks to the presentation.

3. Develop a presentation that incorporates transitions and photographs to create a digital photo album. The focus of this exercise is to use the formatting ribbons and menus to edit, crop, and format photographs of your choice. Develop a minimum of five slides for this presentation.

4. Using the template options available in PowerPoint, create a calendar. Add clip art and text to the dates of importance. How easy is this to read? How easy would it be for an audience to read? When would this type of template be useful?

CHAPTER 5

CREATING EFFECTIVE PRESENTATIONS

In This Chapter

N ow that you have some familiarity with the tools available in presentation software, this chapter focuses on teaching you to use those tools effectively to create a meaningful presentation that can truly make a lasting impression on your audience. You will design, format, and share an example presentation to demonstrate these best practices. Once you complete the chapter, you will be able to:

- Format the Slide Master for your presentation to assign a theme, color scheme, and font set
- Outline an effective presentation using the Notes section of your presentation
- Structure your slides in a logical and complete manner to support the topic on which you are presenting
- Present or share your completed presentation document

5.1 WRITING YOUR VALUE PROPOSITION

Almost every presentation document in existence is a form of sales pitch. Whether it is a research presentation, a marketing proposal, or a presentation about yourself like the one you constructed in the previous chapter, there is some fundamental point that you are trying to convey and you want your audience to agree with what you are saying or at least understand your perspective. The key to constructing a successful presentation is to remember your value proposition or value statement.

A *value proposition* is a concise statement (most commonly associated with business) of the benefits offered by the product or idea under discussion.

Your value proposition is what you have to offer to whoever is viewing your slides or listening to your presentation. This should guide what you include in every slide you create. In fact, you can even state your value proposition in the first slide after the title slide for everyone to see. It should be concise and clear (two sentences at most) so you can easily evaluate each subsequent slide for relevance to that overall message. The difference between an effective presentation and an ineffective presentation is typically determined by the clarity of the message and the quality of the visual display.

5.2 ESTABLISHING A VISUAL STYLE

Part of making your presentation effective is presenting a clear visual style to which the audience can quickly become accustomed; this will allow the audience to recognize the style as you proceed and focus on the content instead of the background. This means choosing an effective style and adhering to that style throughout the presentation. Changing color schemes and backgrounds is distracting; it draws attention to the change instead of what you are trying to highlight. This chapter will guide you through the creation of an effective presentation, no matter what your underlying purpose is. One way to keep your presentation consistent is to use the Slide Master to format your presentation.

A *Slide Master* is a template for all slides within a presentation document. Changes made to a Slide Master will affect all of the slides in the presentation built from that master. Any slide constructed from a Slide Master is considered a child slide to the Slide Master.

Any changes made to the Slide Master will affect all of the slides in the presentation. Using the Slide Master to define your theme, fonts, and colors will give your presentation consistency throughout and will allow you to focus your time and attention on presenting the information rather than on formatting it.

NOTE *Once you become more familiar with PowerPoint, you may want to stop using the Slide Master and change the theme, font, and color scheme directly in the presentation. Even if you end up using it only occasionally, an understanding of the techniques for working with the Slide Master is useful in constructing an effective presentation.*

5.2.1 Modifying the Slide Master

The great thing about using the Slide Master is that it allows you to set up your initial presentation style once and forget about it. All of the other slides that you create within your presentation will be copies of the Slide Master.

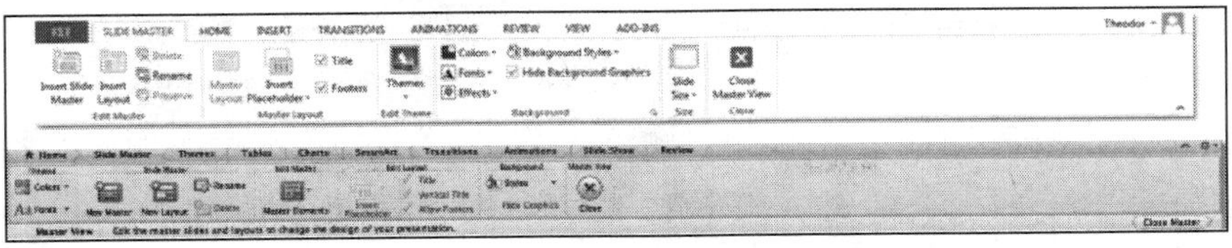

FIGURE 5.1 Slide Master ribbon

Create a new presentation in PowerPoint and save it as *My Sales Pitch.pptx*. To access the Slide Master in PowerPoint 2013, go to the *View* ribbon and click on *Slide Master* under the *Master Views* panel. In PowerPoint 2011, select the *View* menu and choose *Master*; then choose *Slide Master* on the menu that appears.

This opens a new context-sensitive *Slide Master* ribbon, shown in Figure 5.1. The design pane will show a parent slide for all of the different layout options you can choose. Changing the Slide Master will change all of the layout slide masters, which are the children you see in the *Slides/Outline* pane (one for each layout available). Changing any of the layout slide masters changes each individual slide in your presentation with that particular layout.

You will see several placeholder text boxes along the bottom of your Slide Master that typically do not appear in a new slide. These include predefined places to add the date, footer text, and the slide number. Note that in PowerPoint 2013, when the *Slide Master* ribbon is open, the *Design* ribbon disappears; this is because most of the design options that you can apply on a slide-by-slide basis from the *Design* ribbon can be selected and applied on the *Slide Master* ribbon. In PowerPoint 2011, these options are all available on the *Themes* ribbon, which will remain visible whether or not the Slide Master is open.

ACTIVITY 5.1—MASTER SLIDE LAYOUTS

Create a new presentation and save it as *Activity5_1*. With the Slide Master View active, you may notice that you have options for inserting either a new Layout or a new Slide Master. Use each command and compare the resulting insertion into the presentation. When would you use a new Slide Master? When would you use a new Layout? Research this further using the Web if you are not sure. Save your work.

5.2.2 Planning Your Design

Start your presentation with your overall idea and value proposition in mind. The visual style you present in your document will have a big impact on the perception of your idea. You should choose a visual style that supports the message you are delivering and is appropriate for the audience to whom you are presenting. For example, a casual, flashy style with a lot of superfluous animation is not suited to a research presentation because it will give your audience the impression that your graphics are more important than what you have to say. Conversely, a presentation designed for children needs to contain a lot of bright colors or they will quickly become bored and lose interest in what you have to say.

The example project in this chapter is a professional sales pitch. For this type of presentation, you should have a basic idea that you want to convey, which should be supported by all of the slides you add. In this example, the message is simple: "Hot dogs should be the next gourmet food fad." Once you have established the overall message for the presentation, you need to establish the audience for the presentation.

The visual design of a presentation has a large impact on the perceived credibility of the content of the design. In a study about Websites conducted at Stanford University to determine the factors that affect consumer trust, visual appeal was the most often cited reason for whether a site was considered reputable and trusted. The visual clarity of your slides and the visual appeal of the information you present will impact whether your audience trusts what you have to say.

You should take your audience into consideration when planning both your design style and your overall purpose. Putting your ideas in a context that is suited to your audience will help them understand the message you are trying to convey. The background, culture, and experience of your audience will affect their perception of your presentation. Identifying as much information about your audience as possible is critical to successfully delivering your intended message.

The setting in which the audience will experience the presentation will also impact their receptiveness to it. If the occasion is formal, you do not want to select a theme that is juvenile. If it is a casual setting, you do not want your theme to be too rigid and formal. Consider who will be viewing your slides, as well as the message you want to convey. As an example of this, Figure 5.2 shows two versions of the same slide; these have the same content but different styles attached to them. The first would be suited to a more formal occasion but the second would not.

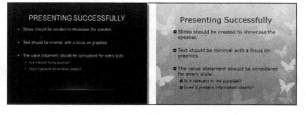

FIGURE 5.2 Alternate designs for the same content

5.2.3 Assigning a Theme

The first step of formatting your master slide is selecting a theme. In PowerPoint, the Theme setting determines the default Font, Color, and Effects settings. In PowerPoint 2013, you select an appropriate theme by clicking the *Themes* icon in the *Edit Theme* panel of the *Slide Master* ribbon and then clicking on one of the preview icons that is displayed. In PowerPoint 2011, these settings are all on the *Themes* ribbon, where you can define the Colors and Fonts settings; there is no equivalent Effects setting.

Selecting the Right Theme for the Venue

When you are choosing a color scheme for your presentation, you need to consider how the presentation will be viewed. If you are showing it on a large screen to an audience, you should consider a color scheme that puts light-colored text over a darker background. A bright background with dark text works well in print, but it can be too harsh to view in a dim room. Similarly, if your presentation is going to be viewed on an individual computer monitor, you should choose a theme that is more akin to text publications. This will also affect your font choices and color scheme, but in PowerPoint these are derived initially from the theme.

NOTE

For the example presentation, you want a style that is going to fit the topic appropriately, so it needs to be something modern that will fit with the business element you are trying to convince to invest in your proposal; it should also not be too formal or it will detract from the spirit of the idea. When you click on a theme, you will see each of the slide templates in the Slides/Outline pane reset to the theme you have chosen, as shown in Figure 5.3. If you do not like the result, you can simply choose another theme.

FIGURE 5.3 Theme selection in PowerPoint 2013

ACTIVITY 5.2—THEME CHOICES

Create a new presentation and save it as *Activity5_2*. Apply a new theme for your presentation where your business is designer cupcakes rather than the gourmet hot dogs used for the example in this chapter. How does the choice of theme change in this case? How does the color palette change? Is your target audience different in this case? Save your work.

5.2.4 Colors, Fonts, and Effects

The next step after choosing a theme is to pick your color scheme. PowerPoint has a significant number of preset color schemes from which you can choose; once you choose a theme, this setting will default to the color scheme that matches that theme. In PowerPoint 2013, you can select any of the preset options from the *Colors* icon (to the right of the *Themes* icon) in the *Background* panel of the *Slide Master* ribbon. The *Colors* menu for PowerPoint 2011 is located in the *Themes* ribbon on the *Theme Options* panel.

You can set the Theme, Color, Font, and Effects settings on the Design *ribbon if you are not using the Slide Master to format your presentation.*

You can also define a custom color scheme by selecting *Customize Colors...* in PowerPoint 2013 or *Create New Theme Colors* in PowerPoint 2011 at the bottom of the list. This process will start with the colors that you have already chosen and allow you to modify them individually; you should be familiar with this menu if you changed the hyperlink color in your presentation in the previous chapter. You can give your new color scheme a name if you want to use it later or save it with the default name (which begins with *Custom 1*). Any custom color schemes you define will appear at the top of the list in the drop-down *Color* menu. You can edit or delete them by right-clicking on the name of the custom color scheme.

Not everyone has the talent to be a professional graphic designer, but there are a few steps you can take to make sure your color scheme works for a presentation. A general guideline is to have two main colors and an accent color. You can use different shades of the main colors, and the two main colors should blend well together. The accent color should be used sparingly and should provide enough contrast to be readable over both of the main colors. You can see a map of complementary and analogous colors on the color wheel in Figure 5.4.

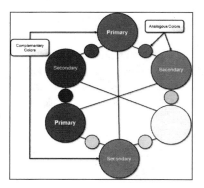

FIGURE 5.4 The color wheel with complementary and analogous colors

There are an almost endless number of usable color combinations, but using two analogous colors and a complementary (or split complementary) color is usually a safe way to construct your palette. Make sure that any text you include is readable above all else and that the tension between the colors does not draw attention away from the content; you can lighten or darken any of the colors to increase or decrease the contrast presented. Remember, the more contrast you have between your text and the background, the clearer your text will be. One color you should avoid is pure red; it is incredibly difficult for a person to look at pure red on a computer or projector screen for any sustained period of time.

You should also choose a font set that is suitable for your presentation; you select a font by clicking on the *Font* icon and selecting one of the options presented. As a general rule, you should never use more than two fonts on a presentation: one for the title to grab attention and one for the rest of the text in the body of your slides. The two fonts should complement each other well, meaning they should not visually clash in style. Readability should be the highest consideration when you are choosing which fonts to use, followed by aesthetic coherence with the overall presentation. Just like with the themes and colors, there are a variety of predefined sets of fonts from which to choose. You can also define your own font set and save it for later use, just as you can with the color scheme.

The fonts in your slides have to be comfortable for people at the back of a room to read if you are going to do a live presentation. A live presentation also means you should stay away from serif fonts. The extra text decorations make it more difficult to read what is on the screen. However, if your presentation is destined for sharing on an individual computer screen, a serif font will work just fine. You can present more stylized text in a presentation for an individual computer screen, but you should never sacrifice clarity and readability.

NOTE *In PowerPoint 2013, you can set the default style for any graphics added to your presentation using the* Effects *icon on the* Theme *panel as well.*

When you select one of the background styles from the menu on the *Background* panel of the *Slide Master* ribbon while you have the default Slide Master (Slide 1) selected, the background choice will be applied to each of the layout slide masters that are linked to it. Most of the layouts will have different elements in the slide than the default blank layout, so it is typically better to select the setting for the background styles in each of the different layout slide masters if you wish to make changes to the default. Each theme will have its own background styles menu choices available. If there is a slide layout for which you do not want the background effects to appear, simply check the box next to *Hide Background Graphics* (or *Hide Graphics* in PowerPoint 2011).

5.2.5 Bullets and Numbering in the Slide Master

Despite the ease of use for bulleted lists in presentation software, bullet points must be used with care. According to Richard Mayer, a leading researcher in educational psychology, the improper use of bullet points can actually cause learning to cease; bullet points can overload the cognitive systems of the brain that normally allow a person to perceive the information with which they are being presented. Because bullet points have no inherent order by definition, the human brain can get lost in them and stop mapping the information. There is no definitive answer on the maximum number of bullet points that should be used in a slide, but the consensus of the research is that three bullet points on a slide does not inhibit understanding if they present clear information.

If you are going to use bulleted or numbered lists in any of your slides, you should set the styles for those in the Slide Master and use them throughout your presentation. Click on the placeholder text box on the Slide Master containing the sample outline text. The styles for the various outline levels will be preset from the theme you selected. You can select whether they should be ordered (using numbers or letters) or unordered (using bullet points) for each level of organization by clicking either the *Numbering* or *Bullets* icon, respectively. You can choose the style for each layer by highlighting the text at the level you want to change and selecting the style for that level.

To open the *Bullets and Numbering dialog box* (shown in Figure 5.5) to make more specific changes, select *Bullets and Numbering* on the right-click menu or select the customization option from the drop-down menu of either the *Bullets* icon or the *Numbering* icon. Here you can change the size relative to the text, the color of the bullets, and the style of the bullets under the *Bulleted* (or *Bullets*) tab. You can also add a picture of your choosing from a file (or from the built-in set of images) as your bullet point by selecting the *Picture* button or you can use one of the special character symbols by clicking the *Customize* button; these options are both under the *Custom bullet* drop-down menu in PowerPoint 2011. On the *Numbered* (or *Numbering*) tab, you can select the outline style you want for the text level and set the starting number or letter by selecting it from the *Starts at* box.

When you are defining the style of your outline for your presentation, you should always keep it as simple and clear as possible. For an unordered list, the text indents should be enough to distinguish the different levels, so you should never need more than one type of bullet. In fact, if you have more than two levels in an unordered list on your slide, the text will become difficult to read. Selecting an image as your bullet point may be novel, but you should only do so if it is not too distracting and it fits with the color scheme and style of the overall presentation. Keep your bullets or numbers the same color within each slide and throughout the entire presentation; changing styles or colors in the same slide just leads to confusion.

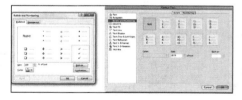

FIGURE 5.5 Bullets and Numbering dialog boxes

5.2.6 Adding and Formatting Slide Footers

Unlike word processing documents, presentations do not contain true headers. The visual impact needs to start at the upper-left corner of the slide. This is where the eye begins viewing the image, so you cannot waste that prime visual space with slide numbers and copyright information. In fact, the only safe place to add this type of information to a slide without causing it to distract the viewer is at the very bottom. The footer is the only area of the slide for which you do not have to worry as much about readability. This is mostly information for the presenter and for later distribution. In fact, any text that is not assisting the presenter (by displaying the slide number, for instance) or needed for copyright information or references should be omitted.

NOTE

If no information is added to the footer placeholders, they will appear as placeholder text boxes in the regular slide design view for your presentation. You can edit the footer information on each slide by clicking on the text just like any other text box.

To make sure no one takes your presentation and uses it as their own, you can add a small copyright notice to your footer. To do this, just type *(c)* into the box; notice that it automatically converts to the copyright symbol (©). Follow this with your name and format the text however you would like it to appear. Remember that this is part of the footer, so it should be small but clear. A font size of 10 to 12 pt is sufficient for the footer but would be otherwise unreadable on a slide; your audience probably will not be able to discern this text.

Add the slide number to the placeholder on the righthand side of the slide for your reference while you are presenting. You may already have a text box with the # symbol; this is the allocated space for the slide number. In PowerPoint 2013, you can insert the slide number manually if it is not already present by placing the cursor in a text box and clicking on the *Insert* ribbon; you will find the *Slide Number* icon on the *Text* panel. You can now format the slide number text to appear the same as the rest of your footer text. The actual number in this placeholder will not be visible until you are in Normal view for your presentation; on the Slide Master, it will appear as <#>.

In PowerPoint 2011, you can add any of the footer elements that you may have removed by selecting the *Insert* menu, clicking on *Master Placeholders*, and choosing the item you want to add. Only the items that are not already included will be available to select. Changing these text boxes does not set the footer on the slides to be visible in your presentation. You can manage the header and footer elements included by selecting the *Header & Footer* icon in the *Insert* ribbon, as shown in Figure 5.6.

To make the footer visible in PowerPoint 2013, you must select the *Header & Footer* icon on the *Text* panel of the *Insert* ribbon. Select the checkboxes that you wish to enable in the *Header and Footer dialog box* that appears, as shown in Figure 5.6. If you want to hide the footer on the title slide of your presentation, check the box next to *Don't show on title slide*. You can reach the Header and Footer dialog box in PowerPoint 2011 by selecting the *View* menu and clicking on *Header and Footer*.

FIGURE 5.6 Header and Footer dialog boxes

5.2.7 Formatting Text on the Slide Master

Any text formatting done to the Master Slide placeholder text boxes will be carried over to the rest of your presentation. Formatting text now in the Master Slide will save you the effort of repeatedly formatting the same elements later when you are writing your presentation content. This not only saves you effort, it also allows you to focus on the content of each slide rather than on formatting.

Center your title and add a shadow to it on the main Slide Master. You should see your changes propagate all the way through the rest of the layout slide masters. To configure the text shadow, select *Shadow Options* from the menu beneath the preset options. This allows you to set how dramatic the shadow effect is. The *Distance* element sets how far away the shadow is from the text, which determines the perceived height of the text over the background.

PowerPoint offers a few text options that are similar to what is available in Word but with a different layout; you can view these in Figure 5.7. One of these options is the *Change Case* icon; this allows you to capitalize the first letter of each word (which is very useful for a title), toggle the case of each letter, or convert all of the letters to either upper- or lower-case. Another tool available here is the *Text Shadow* icon, which lets you add a shadow from the *Font* panel of the *Home* ribbon instead of using the *Text Effects* icon in the *Format* ribbon. There is no icon for superscript or subscript in PowerPoint 2013 as there is in Word. For these effects, you must open the Font dialog box by clicking the expansion icon in the lower-right corner of the Font panel.

PowerPoint 2011 gives you a larger selection of options in the *Font* panel of the *Home* ribbon. These include all of the options available in PowerPoint 2013, along with a few additions. You can add or edit all of the available text effects from the *Home* ribbon, including superscript, subscript, and strikethrough text.

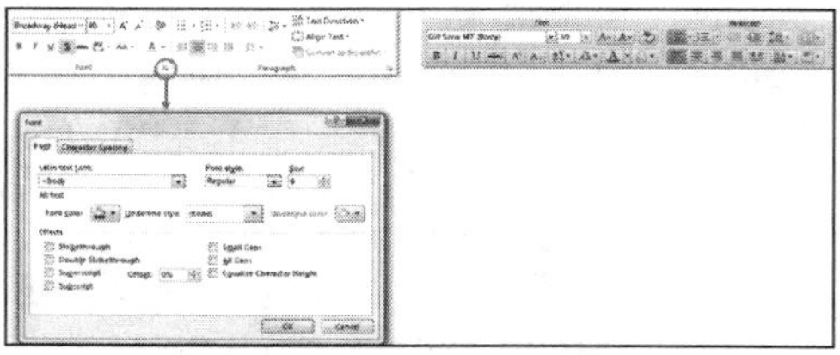

FIGURE 5.7 Font options in PowerPoint

Once you have made the changes to the Slide Master, you should go through each of the layout slides that you are going to use and make any formatting modifications to those that are specific to the layout you need. Unlike the Slide Master parent, anything that you change in a layout slide master will change only the slides built from that layout. This means that changing the format of text in a layout slide master will not make the change in the other layout slide masters. For this reason, it is best to keep any significant text and font style changes to the main Slide Master from which the layout slide masters are created.

5.2.8 Branding Your Slides

If you have a logo for your company or organization, you may want to add it to your slides. You do not want to have to do this for every slide you create, however, and it is best if, once placed, the logo does not change location from slide to slide. Consistency is important to a good presentation, so you should minimize the amount of visual change and misalignment from slide to slide. Slide transitions may mask these changes, but that is not an effective solution to the problem.

You may already have a logo in mind for your presentation, but for the sake of becoming more proficient with the presentation software, you will create one for this project. While the process of creating a logo usually involves hiring an outside expert or going to your organization's graphic designer, here you will use clip art and text boxes to create a sample logo. For a review of how to insert clip art into your slides, you can refer to the previous chapter. Pick a graphic that you like and insert it into the Slide Master parent (Slide 1). You will notice that it propagates all the way through the rest of the layout slides as well. Any elements you add to this slide will appear in every slide of your presentation.

You can now format the graphic with whatever effects you like. Try adding an inner shadow so that the graphic appears to be cut out from the slide background itself. Add a new text box in PowerPoint 2013 by clicking on the *Text Box* icon on the *Text* panel of the *Insert* ribbon. In PowerPoint 2011, you add a text box by selecting the *Text* icon on the *Home* ribbon and choosing *Text Box*. You will need to click and drag your cursor to set the size of this or the active selection will default to the nearest placeholder text box or your newly inserted graphic.

Add whatever name you want for your proposed company. The example here uses "Good Dog Dogs." You can now apply text transformations to make your new company name look more stylized. Try wrapping it in a circle or arching it from one end to the other. Once you have the text looking the way you want, click and drag to select both the clip art image and the text and create a group of these two objects. A completed example is shown in Figure 5.8.

Unfortunately, you cannot just leave your logo sitting in the middle of the slide; it will attract too much of the audience's attention and detract from the content you are going to add. You need to fade it into the background so that it can still be seen but everything else on your slide gets more of the attention. Keep a copy of the full-color logo for your title slide; that is one location where it should be allowed to attract attention. If your logo is new, like the one you just created, this gives your presentation a new identity or branding. If your logo already exists in an organization, you are associating your presentation content with the culture of that organization.

FIGURE 5.8 Example logo

If you want a more advanced logo, you can add multiple layers to it using different pieces of clip art. You can even select certain pieces and use the picture formatting tools to remove the background of the image to make it align with the color of the background beneath it. You can also add drawing elements to your logo, such as the smiley face added to the logo in the example. Whenever you add drawing elements, you must set the color options manually; for instance, there is no single filter that you can apply for a grayscale version.

Copy and paste your full-color logo to the Title Slide layout slide master. Once you have your color copy in place, go back to the Slide Master parent and click on the clip art graphic of your logo. Select the *Format* ribbon (or the *Format Picture* ribbon in PowerPoint 2011). Go to the *Color* (or *Recolor*) icon on the *Adjust* panel and select a color adjustment that sufficiently blends the image into your background. You can see an example of the completed blending in Figure 5.9. If you are using multiple background colors on the layouts for your presentation, you may wish to do this on each of the layout slide masters instead of the Slide Master parent. Just remember to keep the logo in the same location on each slide so it does not change locations as you click through your slides.

FIGURE 5.9 Blended logo

Now you need to alter the text of your logo to fade it into the background along with your graphic. You make these changes using either the *Font* panel of the *Home* ribbon or the options available from the *Format* ribbon. Change any part of your text that is too distracting from the background color to something more appropriate. Anything that creates too much contrast with the background will draw too much attention. You can use the defined colors for your color scheme to help fade the text more effectively. You can generally use the same offset color that you used for the graphic to fade your text. The color names are located along the top row in the Theme Colors area on the drop-down menu of either the *Font Color* icon or the *Text Fill* icon; you can select the fade intensity from the column beneath the color name, as shown in Figure 5.10.

Resize your logo to a reasonable size and adjust the font size of the text to maintain the look that you established when you initially created the logo. One possible location for your logo is at the upper-left corner of the slide; this is where it will receive the most attention,

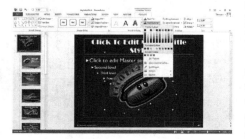

FIGURE 5.10 Using theme colors to blend text

but it also means you will be distracting your audience from the content that is on the slide. Having a sufficiently faded logo in the center of the slide is another possibility, but you have to make sure it does not take away the attention that belongs on the content of the individual slide.

NOTE *If your logo contains too much contrast to filter out using a fade effect, you can add a drawing object rectangle to the slide and set its color and transparency to match the slide background and place it on a layer above the logo but behind the slide content. This will lower the contrast produced by the logo without disrupting the look of the slide. You can see the effect of this in Figure 5.11, which shows the logo with and without the rectangle in place.*

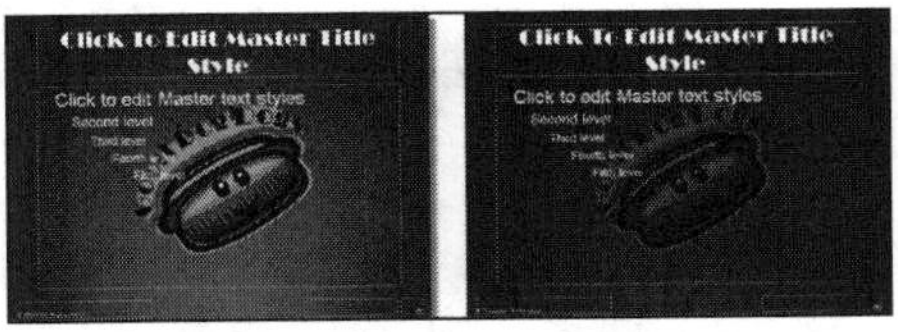

FIGURE 5.11 Effects of a transparent rectangle (shown in the right image) on reducing contrast

Now select the entirety of your logo (the group you made), line it up where you want it on the slide, and send it to the back layer of the slide (*Send to Back*) using the *Arrange* icon. You can also do this using the right-click menu. You should see the placeholder text in front of your faded logo if you have done this correctly, as shown in Figure 5.12. Readers' eyes are naturally drawn to the area of highest contrast in an image, so make sure the text in your text boxes is formatted so it stands out over the logo.

FIGURE 5.12 Completed slide branding

Next you will need to go through each layout of your presentation and choose where the logo belongs and where it does not; this is a yes or no decision since your only option in each of these slides is to select or deselect the *Hide Background Graphics* checkbox (this is found under the *Background* menu in the *Themes* ribbon for PowerPoint 2011). The first stop is the Title Slide layout slide master. Because you should now have both a full-color logo and a faded logo on this slide, you will want to remove the faded copy. To do this, just check the box next to *Hide Background Graphics* (or *Hide Graphics*) on the *Slide Master* ribbon; your faded logo should disappear.

NOTE *You can remove background graphics in the regular design view for your presentation as well, so you will always have the opportunity to remove your logo from the background if it is too distracting; this option is found in the* Design *ribbon for PowerPoint 2013 when you are not viewing the Slide Master. Choose* Format Background *and then check the box to hide the background graphics in the pane that appears. Note that this will also remove the added slide decorations that are added by default to the theme. In PowerPoint 2011, this option is found on the* Themes *ribbon under the* Background *icon.*

Click the *Save* icon to save your work if you have not already done so. Then click the *Close Master View* icon to get back to the regular design view. Now you are ready to start creating your presentation!

ACTIVITY 5.3—CREATING TEMPLATES

If you have put sufficient effort into the formatting of your Slide Master and you wish to use your design later, you can save your presentation as a template file. To do so, click on the *File* menu just as if you were saving the presentation normally. Use the example presentation for this chapter to create a template. Save your file *Activity5_3* and choose *PowerPoint Template* as the document type. Whenever you open a template file such as this one, a new presentation will open based on this style. Give it a try to test the results.

5.3 CONSTRUCTING AN EFFECTIVE PRESENTATION

Remember the value proposition you constructed earlier in the chapter? Now it is time to put it into action! You will create your title slide now and then build your presentation from there.

If you have been following along with the example, your title slide should now contain your new logo. Notice that you cannot edit it from here; it is fixed in place from the Slide Master so you have to change it there if you need to alter its placement. Add a suitable title to your presentation; note that this is not your value statement. The title slide should be a quick placeholder to display as a short introduction to what you have to say, with your name or your organization name as a possible subtitle. The title of your presentation should draw interest as the audience gathers if you are using this for a live presentation; it should give some idea about the topic of the presentation, but it should do so succinctly. Whether or not you have a subtitle is up to you.

5.3.1 Outlining

You should always create an outline for your presentation before you start adding your content. PowerPoint is flexible enough to allow you to move slides and add slides as needed, but you need to make sure your message is delivered successfully throughout your presentation. Your goal in any presentation should be cognitive guidance rather than just information presentation. Without this higher level of information presentation, your audience is unlikely to retain for very long anything that you have shown them.

Cognitive guidance is the presentation of information in a manner that does not overburden the cognitive load (or mental processing capacity) of the viewer or recipient while preserving the meaning of the information; this is a preferable way to share information, as it leads to increased retention and understanding.

Create a rough draft of your outline on paper. You should focus more on the main topics that you want to present as opposed to the specific slides that you are going to include. You may have only a short time to present, so make sure you list out the main topics you absolutely must cover first. These topics should all contribute to the overall purpose of the presentation or they should be removed.

Repeat this process with secondary topics and so forth until you have all of the material listed that you are going to cover. Each time you add a new topic, you should evaluate the relevance to your overall purpose and contribution. If it is not essential or meaningful to your presentation as a whole, it should be removed. You can now use this topic list to structure your presentation by constructing a meaningful map of these topics.

5.3.1.1 Adding Slide Notes

You can start to map your presentation from the rough outline that you have just constructed. Add a slide for each topic that you need to cover. You are not going to construct the actual slides at this point; you will save that for the second pass through your presentation. Instead, you are going to use the *Notes* pane that is visible across the bottom of the interface in *Normal* view to add an outline for what you want to cover in each slide. This is the one area where you can use as many bullet points as needed. You can use the tools available in the Font and Paragraph panels of the *Home* ribbon to format the text in this area, but you cannot add graphic elements like clip art. PowerPoint does not allow you to change the font color here or use text effects, either.

You should use the *Notes* pane for each slide and make an outline of what you want to present. You should not write out everything you are going to say word for word. These should be notes to guide you through your content instead of a set script to follow. If you notice your content for one slide getting too long, you should add a second slide for the topic and split the content between the two. Remember that while your notes will not be visible to the audience when you present, others will be able to view what you have written here when you share the presentation on your computer; keep that in mind when you outline your topics.

NOTE

To help you outline and organize your presentation, PowerPoint 2013 allows you to add section names to your slides to organize them into logical groups. This allows you to make changes to a specific set of slides for one part of your presentation. Your audience cannot see these section names and they do not appear in your outline, so this tool is strictly for your convenience and organization. You can add a section by using the right-click menu or by selecting the Section icon on the Home ribbon. You can use either the right-click menu or the Section icon to change or remove these sections later. In PowerPoint 2011, use the right-click menu or select the Insert menu and then choose Section.

5.3.1.2 Best Practices for Outlining

There are a few guidelines you should always observe in constructing an outline or a map of your presentation. First, you should always get the attention of the audience with the first slide you present; this will be the second slide of your overall presentation. This slide is where the audience will determine how important your topic is to them and whether they will give you their full attention.

NOTE *Your title slide should just be a placeholder before you begin; you can think of it as the curtain that rises before a theater performance. The second slide in your presentation is actually the first slide that you should showcase.*

Your first slide should capture the attention of the audience and interest them in what you have to say. It should be relevant to your presentation, but it should not give away everything you have to say. Give your audience a quick preview of what you are going to show them with your presentation, but do not give them a step-by-step breakdown; you want to emphasize the end goal with this slide. You need to present your main point to the audience three times; this repetition will increase the probability of cognitive recognition in the audience, which will insert the idea into memory. The first occurrence should be at the beginning of your presentation. The second should be as you walk the audience through the problem or opportunity on which your contribution is built. The last iteration of the main idea should be as a summary statement at the end of your presentation.

You need to guide your audience to an understanding of your perspective and show them the value of your main contribution. What you have to say is already important to you, but you need to frame it in such a way that the audience feels it is important to them as well. For example, in a research presentation, you should provide the background on the research problem for which you are presenting a solution; this will allow the audience to see the significance of the research that you have done.

Once you have given the audience your perspective, you should spend the majority of your time presenting what you have to offer. This should be done in a clear manner that the audience can follow from one step or slide to the next. Remember that they are building a cognitive map of this information as you present it, so jumping unexpectedly from a particular topic to something that is unrelated or inconsistent will disrupt that mapping process. Consider the level of prior understanding of your audience to help determine how much information you need to present to them to make it as coherent as possible.

The 10-Minute Mark

NOTE *Humans have a short attention span. Steve Jobs suggested that 10 minutes into your presentation, you need to do something different to focus attention back on yourself and what you have to say. You can provide handouts at this point, show a video, or otherwise get the audience to react to you and reengage.*

When you have demonstrated the main contribution of your presentation, you should emphasize your main point. After all, this is what you came to say, so you need to make sure your audience realizes it. Once you have given your main contribution, you should add any action items that you want the audience to take with them. If they are responsible for some outcome from your presentation, you should deliver your charge to them at this point in your presentation.

Finally, you will add your summary and conclusion. Your summary should be brief and it should state your main contribution for the third time. A single slide should typically be sufficient for a summary; the audience has just experienced your entire presentation, so you should keep the summary short. If you have time for questions, you can add a slide to prompt the audience. A better practice, though, is to transition to a slide with your contact information or the contact information for your organization so people can follow up on their own and then simply ask if they have any questions.

5.3.2 Grabbing Attention in Your First Slide

The first slide of your actual presentation is where you need to grab the audience's attention. If this is a sales pitch and you fail to capture them at the beginning, the likelihood that they will tune in later is slim. There are a lot of different ways to accomplish this. If this is a research presentation, you can build a mystery with an image or a result that the audience wants to see unfolded. With a sales pitch like the one in this chapter, a clear value statement is one way to begin effectively. You should refrain from adding fancy graphics to a text statement here because you do not want to give the impression that you are trying to distract the audience from your main idea.

NOTE
Video can be a great tool to assist a presentation, but it needs to be short and relevant. If you are nervous presenting in front of a crowd, you can include a short video in your first slide to allow you time to calm yourself before you have to start presenting in earnest. You can insert a video in PowerPoint from a file or from a Website. To add a video in PowerPoint 2013, click the Video *icon in the* Insert *ribbon and select the option you want; in PowerPoint 2011, select the* Media *icon on the Home ribbon. The next chapter will give you more specific guidance on including videos in your presentation and formatting and editing them appropriately. If you are constructing a sales pitch, a short video of interviews showing the market need or demonstrating your product is a great way to grab attention at the outset of your presentation.*

On the design side, you should evaluate whether your statement stands out well enough with the color scheme you have chosen. If the contrast is not sufficient to showcase your text, you can change the background style to correct the issue. On any slide in Normal view, you can select the *Format Background* icon on the *Customize* panel of the *Design* ribbon to change your options based on the theme you have selected; this is found under the *Background* icon in the *Themes* ribbon in PowerPoint 2011. Unlike a change in the layout slide masters, a change here will change all of the background styles for the entire presentation. If you need to make this adjustment, you may want to open your Slide Master view and make the design change there instead. Make sure your footer appears correctly on this slide as well. You can see an example of an opening slide in Figure 5.13.

FIGURE 5.13 Example opening slide

5.3.3 Build the Need for Your Presentation

No matter what type of presentation you are developing, the next step is to give the audience the background of why they should care about the problem or opportunity you are attempting to solve or exploit with your presentation. This is true of research presentations, marketing presentations, and simple information presentations. You cannot fully deliver the value of what you are offering if your audience does not share a similar perspective on the situation to which your solution or contribution operates. You have to build the problem statement for them in language they understand so they will at least have enough buy-in to listen to your proposed solution or product.

Always remember who your audience is. Do not waste their time or yours telling them what they already know. Similarly, do not give them a reading assignment with all of the text on your slides, especially if you are presenting in person. The problem formulation should be succinct but clear. The level of detail you add should be determined by the expected audience.

For the example presentation here, it is necessary to build the case for the existence of a market for a new product. Some quick research using the Internet will assist with this, though as always you must evaluate the legitimacy and credibility of any source on the Web. For this example, the Website of the National Hot Dog & Sausage Council (*www.hot-dog.org*) provides statistics regarding the average annual consumption of hot dogs and the locations where they are most consumed to support the establishment of a market for the product being offered. To turn this into a meaningful part of the presentation, you need to pull some impressive data from this and engage the audience with some fun facts. The text of your slides should be easy to read and interesting for your audience, even if they do not have the slightest interest in hot dogs!

Never forget to cite the source of your facts in your presentation. *One way to do this is by using the footer; always be sure to give proper credit for any text or facts that are not your own. At the very least, you should have the full citation of the source in the Notes section of the slide on which you use that information.*

Your text size should never fall below 24 pt font for anything your audience is expected to read. When you have a few key facts to present but they all have a significant amount of text, you can choose a two-column layout to keep the font size high and keep the text on one slide, as shown in Figure 5.14. You can change the layout of the slide by clicking on the *Layout* icon on the *Slides* panel of the *Home* ribbon. In general, you should not use more than two columns for any presentation because it becomes too difficult for the audience to read when there is too much visual information to absorb at once.

FIGURE 5.14 Example of two-column slide layout

Guidelines vary, but the general consensus seems to be a target of three and a limit of five facts or bullet points per slide for a live presentation. Some professional designers, such as Trine Falbe, even argue that each slide should have its own point and more slides are better than cluttered slides; she argues against the use of any bullet points at all. More than numerical restrictions, the clarity and readability of the slide are the most essential qualities. Keep it clear and keep it concise. Your audience needs to be able to digest any text that you have on your slide while listening to what you have to say.

You can be more liberal with the amount of text you include in a standalone presentation, but you must remember that slides are not pages of text. Focus on how to effectively frame the problem that you want to solve or the opportunity you want to exploit. In the example, you want to show that there is a substantial market for your product. You should try to quickly build suspense with the audience so they are interested in the solution and your contribution. Too much background will overshadow what you have to offer and will usually cause the audience to disengage from what you are presenting.

5.3.4 Present Your Main Contribution

The bulk of your presentation should focus on what you have to offer. It should again be clear and concise. It should showcase how you plan to solve the problem at hand or capitalize on the opportunity you just presented. Your audience can usually tell when you are stretching content or wasting time, just as you can tell when someone else is doing it to you, which means you need to keep them engaged while you present what you have to offer.

Keep your slides visually interesting by switching between the different layout options periodically without overwhelming your audience with the change.

You can change the layout of the current slide by clicking the *Layout* icon on the *Home* ribbon and selecting one of the options. If you have constructed your Slide Master well at the beginning, you should only need to make minimal changes to the existing layout slides, which will go a long way toward providing consistency and identity to your presentation.

In this example, additional slides have been added to showcase the planned idea and business model. This type of content should be the bulk of your presentation and should be clear to the audience. Experiment with the different layouts to find what works best for your business case.

5.3.4.1 Effective Visualization

Research has shown that the most effective way for people to retain an idea is for them to experience it visually while it is explained to them. This process is termed *dual-channels*. A person has two separate concurrent brain processes that take in information during a presentation: one is the verbal component and the other is the visual component. This same research has concluded that the visual component is superior (termed the *picture superiority effect*), but the best retention comes from the visual component supporting the verbal component. What this means for your presentation is that you need to make sure your visuals supplement what you are saying instead of substituting for it. In essence, your words will be attached to the image you present in the mind of your viewer. Bullet points and lengthy text do not form a concise image in the mind, meaning this retention will not occur if you oversaturate your slides.

The Notes section can contain as much text as you like, but each slide should present only what is absolutely essential. If you can present the same idea with an image or graph, it is better to do so. You should not use the text on your slides as a crutch for your presentation; you should rehearse your presentation well enough that you recognize the points you have to make based on the visual information of the slide. Find the layout that supports the information you are presenting and tie all of the information on the slide together into a single message as much as possible. If you cannot pull all of the information in your slide into a single coherent thought, you need to split the information into multiple slides.

5.3.4.2 Modifying Layouts

You can change the layout of your slide to any of the preset options by selecting the *Layout* icon on the *Home* ribbon and then selecting which option you want to use. How the information is presented is as important as what information is presented; you can see an example of this in Figure 5.15 where the same information is presented in two different ways. The next two chapters contains more advanced analysis and instructions for including some additional visual elements in your presentation to make it more exciting and interesting.

FIGURE 5.15 The same content in two formats

5.3.4.3 Tips for Success

Keep the following tips for a successful presentation in mind:

- Make your font large enough to read. When in doubt, walk six feet away from your screen and try to read your slide.
- Use bold formatting or an increase in word size to emphasize words and terms in your presentation, but use these sparingly. Italics typically make the text harder to read from a distance, so it should be avoided.
- Never change the font color for emphasis. Too many colors distract the audience and keep the eye from focusing on any one area, making it difficult for the viewer to read the text cohesively.
- If you have different colors of text (such as a hyperlink), keep them within the color scheme chosen for the overall theme.
- Keep your content brief and to the point. You are creating your presentation to engage the audience.
- Create a presentation you would want to see. If it looks bad to you, it will probably look bad to your audience!

5.3.5 Summarize and Conclude

Your summary and conclusion should reemphasize your value statement and your contribution without repeating it word for word. It should be the final bit of information that you leave with your audience for them to consider. One or two slides should be the maximum for your summary and conclusion; you should not be introducing new information here and you do not want to repeat the entire presentation since the audience has just experienced it. The main purpose of the summary and conclusion section is to provide a third repetition of the main point you want to convey.

Your final slide should contain your contact information for anyone who wishes to follow up with you. If you are part of a team, you should include the contact information for all the team members and the areas for which each person is responsible. Make sure your contact information is displayed long enough for anyone in the audience to copy it down if they wish to follow up on your presentation.

NOTE *There are some great SmartArt graphics that allow you to format contact information for multiple contacts clearly and effectively. The topic of inserting and formatting SmartArt is covered in the next chapter.*

It is common to include a slide seeking questions from the audience. Your venue should dictate whether this is allowed or feasible. If you decide to include such a slide, you may want it as a precursor to your contact information or concurrently with your contact information. The slide containing your contact information is the one that should linger on the screen for a live presentation while you field questions because it will allow audience members to copy down your information if they do not wish to ask questions in public or if there is not enough time to get to them.

<u>NOTE</u> *If you are sharing a presentation document as a supplement after you have presented it, you should adjust the slide for questions to direct the viewer to the person who can answer them. For instance, you would want to change the text "Questions?" to something like "If you have questions, you can contact..." This small change will increase the professionalism of the result.*

Now that you have completed your presentation, you should view it to make sure it is coherent and presents the message you want with the clarity it needs. You also need to check the alignment of your images and drawings to make sure they are correct.

FIGURE 5.16 The effect of alignment on a graphic

Misalignment can be distracting to your audience and can ruin the impact your graphic would have otherwise had; an example of the effect alignment has on a graphic is shown in Figure 5.16. Your design work may be complete, but there are several things you still need to do before your new masterpiece is ready for public consumption. If you are giving a live presentation, you will need to prepare your timings and rehearse. If you are sharing your presentation via the Web or another mechanism to present on an individual computer, you can either record your narration or set up your presentation so it plays automatically with the timings that you have defined.

5.4 PRESENTING YOUR MASTERPIECE

Your presentation is a performance piece. Like any theater performance, you need to make sure you rehearse what you have to say so you can present it coherently and with authority. This applies whether you are in front of a live audience or recording your narration. You should never find yourself in a situation where you are reading the slide contents to the audience; doing so will cause them to disengage from what you have to say and will give you the appearance of being unprepared. Whether or not you like being in front of an audience, you should just be yourself. You do not need to pretend to be more serious than you are.

You, not the slides you are presenting, will engage the audience. You should not be afraid to make them smile and you do not have to be perfect; in fact, the audience will accept you better if you come to them prepared but present as yourself. Most presentation software gives you a variety of options for practicing your slide timing, and PowerPoint gives you the option of directly recording narration for your slides. You can also broadcast your presentation live and even save it as a video to share if you are using PowerPoint.

5.4.1 Live Presentations

You should go through your notes enough times to be familiar with the content you are presenting. This is true whether you have created the presentation or you are just presenting it on someone else's behalf. Your audience will disengage if you start reading the slides to them, so you should have an idea of what you are saying without using the written text on the slide as a script. You should know your presentation well enough that you recognize the topics you need to cover on a particular slide based on the slide graphics alone.

You can practice your slide timing using the *Rehearse Timings* icon on the *Slide Show* ribbon. This will start your presentation in Slide Show view with a clock and a small interface for moving your slide show forward or repeating the current slide, as shown in Figure 5.17. PowerPoint 2011 gives you a larger interface called Presenter view (also shown in Figure 5.17), where you can see your notes as well. This will tell you how long you are spending on each of your slides, which is helpful information if you need to present within a fixed time limit. When you are finished with your rehearsal, you will be prompted to save your slide timings. If you choose this option, your slide show will stay on each of the slides for the set amount of time that you took to cover the material and will switch to the next slide automatically when that amount of time has passed.

If you have multiple monitors attached to your computer, such as the regular display monitor and a digital projector, you can select *Use Presenter View* on the *Slide Show* ribbon when you wish to present. This option allows you to select which monitor will display the show in Slide Show view and which monitor will show the special Presenter view, which contains the slide show and your Notes section for the current slide. Using the Presenter view can be helpful when you are making your presentation, especially if you encounter a particularly difficult topic and want to make sure you present the correct details. However, you should not rely on the Notes section of your presentation to speak to your audience. It is always better if you know your presentation well enough to talk to the audience without continually referring to your notes or your slides.

When you are in Slide Show view (or the local Reading view equivalent) in PowerPoint 2013, you can use your mouse as a laser pointer on the slide to highlight information. The default behavior of the mouse in this view is to advance the slide just like the spacebar or the right arrow key; however, when you hold down the *Control (Ctrl)* key and left-click the mouse, the cursor will appear as a laser point on the screen for as long as you hold the left button down. You can record this mouse movement during the default recording process that is explained in the next section. The color of the laser pointer cursor can be set in the dialog box that appears when you click the *Set Up Slide Show* icon in the *Slide Show* ribbon. Figure 5.18 shows the dialog box and the pointer in action.

If you need to mark up your slides to highlight information, both PowerPoint 2013 and PowerPoint 2011 give you the

FIGURE 5.17 Rehearse Timings interface

FIGURE 5.18 Using the mouse as a laser pointer

option to change your mouse cursor to a pen. To access this, simply right-click on your slides in Slide Show view and select the *Pen* option. This will change your mouse to a pen for the current slide. You will have to advance the slide using the spacebar or arrow key, but the default mouse behavior will be restored on the next slide.

5.4.2 Recording Narration

If you are sharing your presentation on an individual computer screen, you may find it beneficial to record narration instead of just sharing the slides themselves. In fact, if you have constructed the slides successfully, you will need narration to support them. In PowerPoint, you can easily record narration using the *Record Slide Show* icon. This will prompt you for preferences and allow you to select whether you want to record your narration from the beginning of the presentation or from the current slide. After you have set your options, you will be presented with an interface that looks just like the rehearsal interface except it includes an icon to pause and resume the recording.

NOTE *In order to record sound on your machine, you must have a sound card and a microphone connected to the audio input line of your computer. Most computers have a default internal microphone that you can use automatically, but not all of them do!*

When you have completed your recording, you can review the narration by selecting the Slide Show view (you can do this quickly by pressing *F5*). The narration will play just like the animation and transitions in the preview mode. The individual narrations will appear as a small audio icon in the lower-right corner of the slide and they will play by default when the slide is reached in Slide Show view. If you do not want to keep a particular narration in PowerPoint 2013, select *Clear* from the drop-down options under the *Record Slide Show* icon. In PowerPoint 2011, you can record the presentation again to save over the previous narration.

5.4.3 Sharing Your Presentation

You can share your presentation document just like any other file. It can be emailed or placed on transferrable media to share. Be aware, however, that you must include any linked media along with the native presentation document or the media will not be transferred.

Linked media is any file that has been added to the presentation by reference that is not embedded into the presentation document itself. An example of this is a file that opens as a result of an action being activated.

In PowerPoint, you have the option to save your presentation document as a PowerPoint Show. To do this, use the *Save As* function and select the document type *PowerPoint Show* (.ppsx). If you save your document in this manner, it will open in Slide Show view whenever a user clicks on its icon. The presentation cannot be modified in this format, but the viewer does not have to have PowerPoint installed to view the show; the presentation uses the Microsoft PowerPoint Viewer software instead. This document type is a good choice if you do not want anyone to see the notes you have attached and you want the viewer to experience the presentation as you have scripted it. The drawback of this format is that included elements like video are dependent on the properties of the host machine the viewer is using and may not work as you intended.

The latest versions of PowerPoint have overcome this limitation by providing the ability to save your presentation as a video. In PowerPoint 2013, you can save your presentation as a video by clicking on the *File* menu and selecting *Export* and then *Create a Video*. This will open a new menu of options where you can select the video resolution you want, whether you want to use recorded narration and timings, and if you want to spend only a set amount of time on each slide. Once you have selected your options, click the *Create Video* icon beneath the settings, as shown in Figure 5.19. This will open the Save As dialog box where you can save the presentation as a *Windows Media Video* (.wmv). This format will include all of your content in the video except Apple QuickTime movies and elements that require third-party software to display. You must also update linked media from any Office 2007 (or prior) content that is still included in the presentation for it to be included in the video.

PowerPoint 2011 offers you the ability to save your presentation as a *Movie* (.mov) through the regular Save As function. You can adjust the settings for your movie by clicking the *Options* icon on the Save As dialog box with *Movie* selected in the *Format* box.

PowerPoint also offers you the option of broadcasting your presentation in a live synchronous environment. This service is available for all PowerPoint 2013 and PowerPoint 2011 users, but it does require you to have a Windows ID. Clicking the *Present Online* icon in PowerPoint 2013 or the *Broadcast Slide Show* icon in

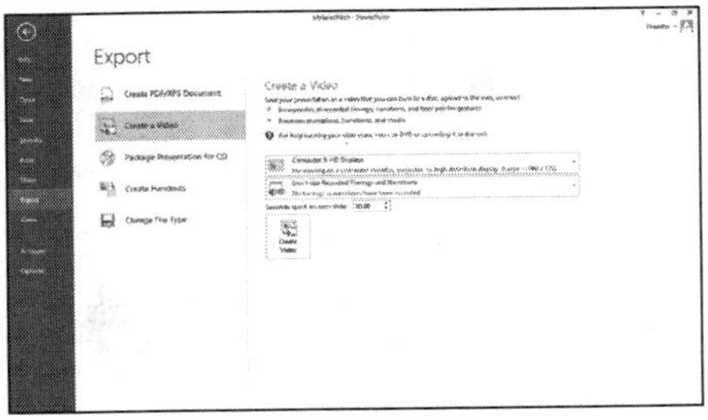

FIGURE 5.19 Create a Video option in PowerPoint 2013

PowerPoint 2011 on the *Slide Show* ribbon will prompt you to log in using your Windows ID and password (if you are not already connected to your account in PowerPoint 2013). The software will then generate a public link you can share that can be used by up to 50 viewers to access your presentation live over the Internet whether or not they have PowerPoint installed. This will play your presentation in a special Broadcast view, which allows you to control your presentation as you would in a live setting. Once you have finished your presentation, click *End Broadcast*; this will terminate any viewer connections to your presentation and the link will no longer be valid. You should note that the only audio that will be shared in this format is what is recorded within the presentation.

ACTIVITY 5.4—EXPORTING YOUR PRESENTATION

Using the presentation you constructed in this chapter, you will export it as a video. Follow the instructions given for your version of PowerPoint and note the options that are available for the video settings. Save your video as *Activity5_4*. Play back your video to see the end result.

CHAPTER SUMMARY

This chapter focused on the effective use of presentation software to impact your audience and assist you in presenting what you have to say in the best possible manner. Using a Slide Master and predefined formatting options, you can quickly create the design of your presentation to allow you to focus on the content, which is by far the most important aspect of any presentation. You should also now have an understanding of how to share and present your new slide show. You can see the completed slides for the chapter example in Figure 5.20. This should give you a comparison for the structure and presentation of your own work. The next chapter will focus on additional graphic enhancements and media you can add to enliven your presentation even more.

FIGURE 5.20 Completed chapter example slides

CHAPTER KNOWLEDGE CHECK

1. The _____ is the option that allows you to set up your initial presentation style.
    a. Slide list
    b. Content

c. Slide Master

d. Theme menu

2. Readability should be the highest consideration when you are choosing which fonts to use in your presentation, followed by aesthetic coherence with the overall presentation.

   a. True

   b. False

3. You should start your presentation with your overall _____ and your _____ proposition in mind.

   a. Idea, value

   b. Value, business intelligence

   c. Idea, proposal

   d. Idea, simple

4. Creating too much contrast with the background will draw too much visual attention.

   a. True

   b. False

5. You can practice your slide timing using the _____ icon on the *Slide Show* ribbon.

   a. Rehearse Timings

   b. Animation Timing

   c. Duration

   d. Advanced Slide Timing

Practice Exercises

1. Using the skills learned in this chapter, develop a 10-slide presentation on a topic of your choice using all three of the important considerations provided: the idea, value proposition, and consistency. Use the Slide Master to develop a consistent presentation by using a built-in theme and choosing formatting and colors that provide aesthetic coherence.

2. Using a fictional business, create a value proposition for a product you are launching. This should be a statement of no more than two sentences that outlines the benefits offered by your business' product or service. Create three alternate slides to present this information. Which of these is most effective? Why is this the case?

3. Use a value proposition to help you create a PowerPoint presentation for your grand opening. Design a presentation that will let the attendees know about your new business and what it offers that your competitors do not offer. Make sure to establish the presentation's visual style using

a slide master. Write a summary of your theme choices. Make sure to include the elements that will affect where and how you will be presenting your PowerPoint presentation. For instance, you might want to discuss your chosen venue's lighting and acoustic setup which will inevitably determine any constraints.

4. To ensure that you maintain your audience's focus, develop your 10-minute plan. If your presentation you created for your business is shorter than ten minutes, use the midway mark. Devise a plan to regain or refocus your audience's attention during your presentation. Describe your plan and develop any additional materials needed.

CHAPTER 6

ADDING COMPLEX MEDIA IN PRESENTATION SOFTWARE

In This Chapter

Now that you are familiar with the concepts of creating presentation documents, you can improve the impact you have on your audience with the use of advanced media. This chapter covers how to add more complex media elements into your slides and where and how to use them effectively. This includes the use of tables, charts, and animation. When you have completed the chapter, you will be able to:

- Add advanced media to your presentation, including sound, video, tables, and graphs
- Recognize and use different chart types in your presentation to accurately convey information to your audience quickly
- Create animation within your slides and change the timing and start conditions for your animation effects

6.1 ADDING ADVANCED MEDIA

A plethora of media options can be embedded into presentation software beyond the images and clip art that have been discussed so far. The key to using media effectively in your presentations is to make sure you are using it with the purpose and audience in mind. It is easy to overdo the amount of media in presentations, so you should restrict the media elements on each slide. For instance, if you add a video to your slide, the video should stand alone. If you have a table, it will be difficult enough for your audience to read, so you can add slight graphic enhancements to emphasize your point, but you should stay away from distracting elements like clip art on the same slide. Keep visibility and focus in mind for your audience.

If you are distributing your presentation on the Web or presenting it on a machine that is not your own, you want to keep the file size of the presentation document in mind as well. Large files will not download as quickly and cannot be as easily shared; your audience may not have the patience to download a large file from a Website if they are only casually interested in a subject, which means they will not even give your presentation a chance if it is too big. By default, video and sound take up more file space than images and static text. Text and drawing objects do not require a lot of memory to store. Make sure the media you add is necessary or serves a purpose; otherwise, it should be removed. There is no absolute maximum size, but you should take care not to go too far over 2 MB for a casual presentation shared on the Internet. Most Internet connections can handle that amount of information in a short enough time that the user will not become frustrated while the presentation downloads. Throughout this chapter, you will modify and enhance the *My Sales Pitch* presentation you have been working on already.

6.1.1 Sound and Video

PowerPoint offers a lot of options for inserting sound and video into your presentation. Any sound that you add should be minimal, however. Harsh sound is disrupting to a viewer, especially when fade-in effects are not used. Other than narrating the slides in a saved presentation, you should use sound only when it makes a strong point that a visual element cannot make. To add audio to your presentation in PowerPoint 2013, click the *Insert* ribbon and then the *Audio* icon; from here you can select Online Audio to access the Office.com library. To add audio in PowerPoint 2011, click the *Media* icon on the *Home* ribbon and select *Audio from File.* You can choose an audio file either from a file on your local machine or from the clip art collection.

A *fanfare* is a single-use audio file for a slide with a big reveal, such as the venue for your first business location. You should only use it once to get the attention of your audience and it should be short. This only works in a more casual setting; you should not use an audio interruption in a formal setting. You can find a suitable audio clip using the Office.com Clip Art window in PowerPoint 2013 and entering the keyword *fanfare* in the *Search for* box. Once you have selected your sound (you can preview sounds by holding your mouse cursor over each sound icon), you will see an icon that looks like a speaker appear in your slide. This is the action icon for the sound. When you select the action icon for an audio file in PowerPoint 2013, two context-sensitive Audio Tools ribbons appear, as shown in Figure 6.1. The two ribbons are the

FIGURE 6.1 Audio icon and Audio Tools ribbons in PowerPoint 2013

Format ribbon (which contains the familiar formatting tools you have seen used for images) and the *Playback* ribbon. PowerPoint 2011 has only the *Audio Format* ribbon, which combines the formatting options with a small number of additional features from the equivalent *Playback* ribbon in PowerPoint 2013; the audio editing options in PowerPoint 2013 are not available in PowerPoint 2011. When you select the action icon for the audio file in your slide, a pop-up interface appears that lets you preview the file using the play button and set the volume.

The *Playback* ribbon (which is only available in PowerPoint 2013) has a number of useful features. The Set Bookmark feature lets you set where you want to start the audio clip or where you want to stop it if it should play from the beginning. You can

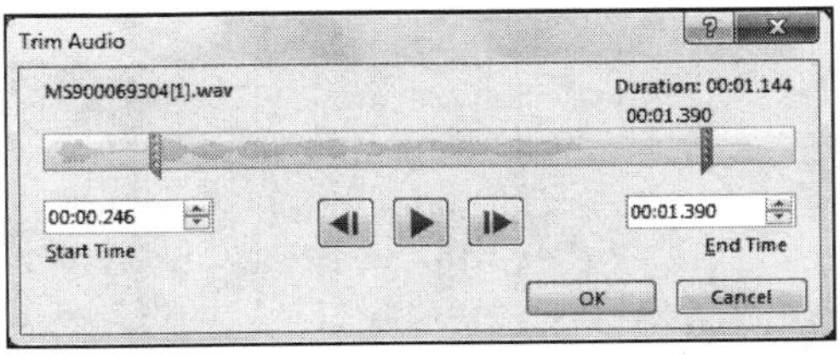

FIGURE 6.2 Trim Audio dialog box in PowerPoint 2013

then use the *Trim Audio* icon to access the *Trim Audio* dialog box, shown in Figure 6.2, in which you can cut off excess parts of the sound file that you do not want to play.

You can click and drag the green start slider and the red end slider to whatever section of the audio you want to keep. Having the bookmark in place will simply let you slide directly to that mark. You can also preview the audio in the *Trim Audio* dialog box, so it is possible to complete the same task without using bookmarks as you gain more experience. Click *OK* when you are finished to apply the trim. This process does not remove the trimmed ends from the file, so you can go back into the *Trim Audio* dialog box to make changes later.

You use the *Playback* ribbon in PowerPoint 2013 to set the start trigger, or what causes the audio to begin; this can be when the slide appears or it can be triggered manually. Setting the Start option to *Play Across Slides* means the audio will continue even after the slide on which it was started is changed in Slide Show view. You can also set a duration for the Fade In and Fade Out options, which determines how long it takes the sound to start playing from zero volume to its set level or from its set level to zero volume, respectively. PowerPoint 2011 allows you to set the start trigger in the *Audio Format* ribbon by setting a value in the *Start* field.

NOTE *You can alter the volume setting for the clip, but be aware that this will be a relative value to the overall volume setting of the machine on which the slide show is being presented.*

Now it is time to add a video to the presentation. The video is going to be on the attention-grabbing first slide even before the value statement that you constructed. As this presentation is your first introduction to the audience, it should be something that gets their attention and introduces the subject of the presentation. Insert a new slide after the title slide with the default layout; this is where you will insert your video.

PowerPoint offers the ability to insert a movie from the embed code of a Website in HTML format. Doing so does not give you the full options for video editing and will instead import the player that is used on the Website to display the content. It is usually a better choice to use a downloaded video in PowerPoint because you have more control over how it looks and how it plays. There are also a lot of copyright issues you need to consider with the use of any media file taken from the Web.

To insert a video in PowerPoint 2013, select the *Insert* ribbon and then choose the *Video* icon. You can also insert a video from a file using the *Insert Media Clip* quick link in a placeholder text box for content. The Clip Art library has some options available, but they probably are not worth using in the first 30 seconds of your presentation. You should ideally have a specific video in mind for this first slide. For this example, use the file *MySalesPitchVideo*. Once you have chosen your file, you will see the two context-sensitive *Video Tools* ribbons shown in Figure 6.3. The two ribbons include a *Format* ribbon, which is the same for audio and images, and a *Playback* ribbon that is almost identical to the audio equivalent. PowerPoint 2011 allows you to add a video from the *Media* menu in the *Home* ribbon; this provides you with the context-sensitive *Format Movie* ribbon, which has all of the formatting commands and a subset of the *Playback* ribbon options in PowerPoint 2013. When you select a video image in PowerPoint, you will see a small pop-up menu that allows you to play the file, adjust the audio, and move among any chapters that exist in the file.

Most of the configuration options for video are the same as they are for audio. PowerPoint 2013 allows you to configure Fade In and Fade Out effects. Whenever you use a Fade In effect, though, the video screen will fade from solid black and zero volume; similarly, a Fade Out effect will fade to a solid black screen and zero volume. The Trim Video interface (again available only in PowerPoint 2013) has the same functionality as the Trim Audio interface, but it includes a preview of the video as well as the sound.

Whenever you are showing a video, it should take up as much of the screen as it reasonably can within your theming. You can remove the placeholder text box for a title to increase the screen size of the video and make the slide more visually interesting by selecting a unique look for the player. An example of this is shown in Figure 6.4.

FIGURE 6.3 Video Tools Playback ribbon and pop-up Video menu in PowerPoint 2013

FIGURE 6.4 Formatted example of a video within a slide

6.1.2 Tables

Just as in word processing software, tables are a great way to provide visual organization for information. The difference between the use of tables in word processing documents and in presentations is the readability of the information in a table. In a written document, it is easy for the viewer to absorb the information and identify the relevant elements. This is not the case with a presentation. Anytime you use a table, you should either limit the text so the audience can read the entire table quickly or highlight a certain element of the table with additional visual notation so the audience knows where to look. Adding too many rows and columns turns the table into an eye chart for the audience at the back of the room. Remember that when an audience is reading, they are not listening to the speaker.

FIGURE 6.5 Insert Table dialog box from quick links in PowerPoint 2013

The next element to add to the sales pitch presentation is a short version of the menu. Add a new slide to your presentation after the slide that shows a graphic of a sample product. There are several ways to insert tables into a slide. The first is to use the quick links from one of the content placeholder text boxes. When you click the *Table* icon, a small Insert Table dialog box appears, as shown in Figure 6.5, in which you can select the number of rows and columns you want for your table. When you have set these values, click *OK*.

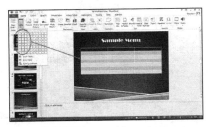

FIGURE 6.6 Table menu from the Insert ribbon in PowerPoint 2013

Another alternative in PowerPoint 2013 is to use the *Insert* ribbon and click the *Table* icon. This opens a pop-up menu that allows you to highlight the number of rows and columns you want your table to have, as shown in Figure 6.6. You can access the same Insert Table dialog box from this menu that you could from the quick links on the placeholder text box. In PowerPoint 2011, you can add a table from the quick links or by selecting the *Table* ribbon and choosing the *New* icon; this will open the same pop-up menu where you can choose the number of rows and columns for your table.

The table in this example has four rows and three columns. Once you have selected the number of rows and columns for the table, you can start to format the table itself. Clicking and dragging any of the corner grab points or the midpoint grab points resizes the entire table. Clicking and dragging any of the vertical or horizontal lines within the table resizes the table cells. When you select a table in PowerPoint 2013, two context-sensitive *Table Tools* ribbons appear, as shown in Figure 6.7. The *Tables* ribbon is always present in PowerPoint 2011, but when you select a table, the *Table Layout* ribbon appears.

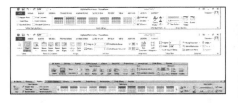

FIGURE 6.7 Table Tools ribbons in PowerPoint

The *Design* ribbon for the Table Tools in PowerPoint 2013 allows you to set up how your overall table will look; these options are found on the standard *Tables* ribbon in PowerPoint 2011. Checkboxes let you specify whether you want particular rows highlighted in a different color than the rest. The example uses the *Header Row* and *Banded Rows* options to increase the distinction between the elements of the table. You can select any of the predefined styles from the *Table Styles* panel, and you can also set the *Shading* color, *Borders*, and *Effects* options for the cell you currently have selected. The *Draw Borders* panel lets you define the thickness and color of the borders for the currently selected cell (or cells).

The *Layout* ribbon for the Table Tools (or the *Table Layout* ribbon in PowerPoint 2011) allows you to modify the size of the selected cells, the size of the overall table, and the placement of text within the cells, as well as add or remove rows and columns. You can also use Merge Cells to merge multiple neighboring cells into a single cell of the table or Split Cells to split a single cell into multiple cells. The *Distribute Rows* and *Distribute Columns* icons will attempt to give each of the cells in your table an equal division of the height or width of the table, respectively. A completed example for the menu table is shown in Figure 6.8.

FIGURE 6.8 Completed table example

Remember that your table needs to be readable above all else, so if there is a particular cell or result you want to highlight, you can modify the look of that cell so it draws more attention. You can also add a drawing object like a circle to emphasize to your audience that they should pay attention to that particular element of the table. Long tables can interrupt the flow of a presentation just like a long list of bullet points, so make sure you use tables sparingly.

ACTIVITY 6.1—TABLES

Create a new presentation and save it as *Activity6_2*. Add a new slide to the presentation using the Default layout. For the first slide, choose the Table icon from within the content placeholder. Add a table using three columns and three rows. Add data to the table and view the slide in Slide Show View. How clear is the information in the table? What are some ways to alter the format of the table to make the data clearer to the audience? Be sure to save your work.

6.1.3 SmartArt

SmartArt is a tool that is available in most of the Office applications; it converts bulleted text (typically with two outline levels) into a professional-looking graphic image. The styles and format for SmartArt are all predefined, but you can alter the color scheme to match your presentation and change certain style attributes.

One possible use of SmartArt is to create a graphic for contact information that can include text and images for multiple people, such as if there is more than one author of the presentation or if multiple people or groups should be listed for possible follow-up after the presentation. For the sales pitch example, you are going to use SmartArt to replace the existing contact information slide (which was created in the example project in the previous chapter).

Create a new slide at the end of the presentation with the default layout and add a title (you can use *Questions*? just like you did on your previous contact page). To insert a SmartArt graphic in PowerPoint 2013, select the *Insert* ribbon and choose *SmartArt*; you can also use the SmartArt quick link within the content placeholder text box. This will open the *Choose a SmartArt Graphic* dialog box shown in Figure 6.9. From here, you can select the type of graphic you want to create. In PowerPoint 2011, you can open the *SmartArt* ribbon and choose the graphic type you want to use. For the example, choose *Vertical Curved List*

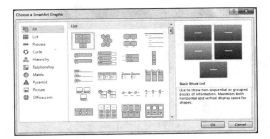

from the List category. When you insert and select a SmartArt graphic, a small window appears in which you type the text of your graphic in bulleted outline form. The outline level of the text determines where it is placed on the graphic.

When you select the SmartArt graphic, you will also see two context-sensitive SmartArt tools ribbons; these are the *Design* ribbon and the *Format* ribbon. The *Format*

FIGURE 6.9 Choose a SmartArt Graphic dialog box in PowerPoint 2013

ribbon is similar to the other formatting ribbons you have already seen; you can change the style of the drawing object within the SmartArt graphic selected and you can change the text formatting for any selected text. An example of the active *Design* ribbon is shown in Figure 6.10 (along with the SmartArt text entry box for the example).

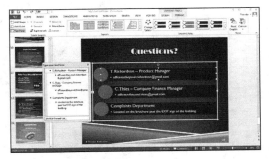

FIGURE 6.10 Example SmartArt text entry box and SmartArt Tools Design ribbon in PowerPoint 2013

The *Design* ribbon in PowerPoint 2013 contains several tools specific to SmartArt. The *Create Graphic* panel provides you with tools to add to your graphic or rearrange elements. The *Add Shape* icon allows you to insert new graphic objects for your SmartArt and select their placement (relative to the currently active bullet point or object). You can also show or hide the *Text* pane using the *Text Pane* icon. The *Promote* and *Demote* icons allow you to change the outline level of the selected bulleted text, and Move Up and Move Down allow you to adjust the order of the objects (you can use these within the *Text* pane as well). In the *Layouts* panel, you can change the SmartArt graphic within the same style as the current graphic; if you need to change the entire category, you must create a new SmartArt graphic.

NOTE *Some SmartArt graphics will have placeholder elements to add a picture. To add pictures, click the picture icon in the graphic or the picture icon next to the text in the* Text *pane. You can edit the image and its properties with the same* Picture Tools Format *ribbon that you use for any other image.*

The *Colors* icon lets you adjust the color scheme of the graphic, and the *SmartArt Styles* panel allows you to make changes to the look and feel of the entire graphic at once. Reset Graphic sets the style back to the default settings. Finally, the *Convert* icon allows you to change the SmartArt graphic into regular drawing objects and text. The new slide with the SmartArt graphic will be used as your new contact slide, but do not delete the old contact slide yet; you will use it in a later section of this chapter.

These functions are all available in PowerPoint 2011, but their locations are split between the *SmartArt* ribbon and the *Text* pane. The promotion, demotion, and ordering icons are on the *Text* pane, while the formatting and style options remain on the *SmartArt* ribbon, where you can change the layout of your graphic as well. The *Text* pane will appear as a small clickable icon beside the graphic when it is hidden so you can reactivate it from there.

ACTIVITY 6.2—SMARTART

Create a new presentation and save it as *Activity6_2*. Add two slides to the presentation using the Default layout. For the first slide, choose the SmartArt icon from within the content placeholder. Choose one of the graphics and add text to complete it. For the second slide, use the Insert menu to add SmartArt and choose a different type of graphic. Add text to complete this graphic. How did the process differ for the two examples of SmartArt that you added? How does the text map to the SmartArt elements in each example you chose? Be sure to save your work.

6.2 CHARTS

Charts are another great way to present data quickly. A chart can display a lot of complex data in a single visualization that may take a significant amount of text to explain. In PowerPoint, charts are built from Excel spreadsheet documents. Do not be intimidated if you have never used Excel before, as the example here just uses basic information. You will explore different types of charts in this section and you should take the time to try to recreate the charts in a presentation using the data provided.

6.2.1 Adding Charts in PowerPoint

To insert a chart in PowerPoint 2013, use the *Insert* ribbon and select *Chart*. In PowerPoint 2011, select the *Charts* ribbon and choose the type of chart you want to insert. You can also add a chart from the quick links *Insert Chart* icon from any content placeholder text box. This opens the *Insert Chart* dialog box for PowerPoint 2013, shown in Figure 6.11; in PowerPoint 2011, this just activates the *Charts* ribbon.

For now, select a simple *Line Chart* from the list and click *OK*. This will open a small Excel window within PowerPoint, as shown in Figure 6.12. The data that will be used to construct your line graph is displayed in the spreadsheet in Excel. This example will show a simple line indicating projected sales for the first three months of operation. You can resize the data used in the chart by dragging the blue indicator in Excel that encloses the data used by the chart.

Since the summer months see the largest sales for hot dogs, the business will launch in June. Therefore, enter *June*, *July*, and *August* for the Category names in Column A of the spreadsheet. Then add the word *Sales* in place of "Series 1." For the data values, June will have 1 sale (cell B:2), July will have 250 (cell B:3), and August will have 5000 (cell B:4). The completed data entry and the proper position for the blue indicator point are shown in Figure 6.12. Once you have completed the data entry, close Excel. You can reopen it from the *Design* ribbon for Chart Tools by selecting the *Edit Data* icon, which will allow you to either open the small window within PowerPoint or open Excel fully.

PowerPoint should now return to its former window size and you can see the three context-sensitive *Chart Tools* ribbons that appear as shown in Figure 6.13. The *Format* ribbon that appears here should be familiar to you by now; this allows you to set the text effects and shape effects of the different chart elements. For instance, you can add a shadow to the sales line you have created or add text effects to the chart information, but you should not sacrifice clarity and readability to add effects.

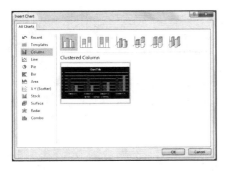

FIGURE 6.11 Insert Chart dialog box in PowerPoint 2013

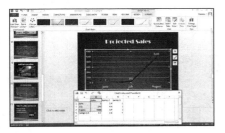

FIGURE 6.12 Completed chart data entry

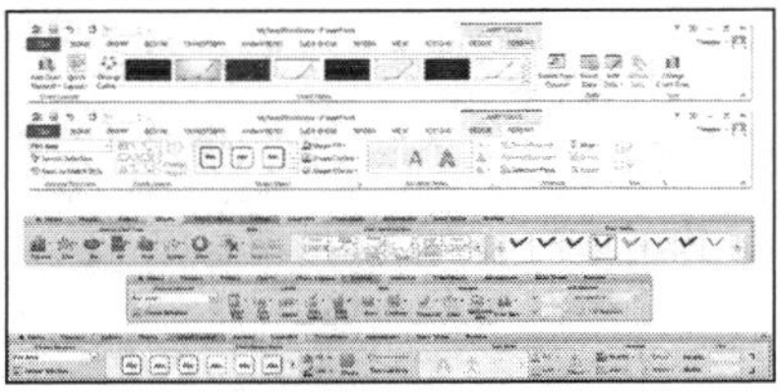

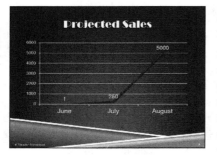

FIGURE 6.13 Context-sensitive Chart Tools ribbons

The *Design* ribbon for Chart Tools (the standard *Charts* ribbon in PowerPoint 2011) allows you to set the look and feel of the chart. There are a number of preset layouts and styles that you can select to display your data from the *Chart Layouts* panel and the *Chart Styles* panel. You can also use the *Edit Data* icon (*Edit* in PowerPoint 2011) on the *Data* panel to open the Excel spreadsheet to make any changes to the data on which the chart is based.

The *Layout* ribbon for Chart Tools (or the *Chart Layout* ribbon in PowerPoint 2011) allows you to change the display elements of the chart. You can primarily change how much visual information is displayed on the chart using this ribbon. The options on this ribbon differ for PowerPoint 2013 and PowerPoint 2011. Some of the functionality for the PowerPoint 2011 ribbon is part of the menus beside the chart in the slide itself in PowerPoint 2013.

For the example, select the *Data Labels* icon and choose *Above*; you can find this option in the *Design* ribbon for Chart Tools in PowerPoint 2013 under the *Add Chart Elements* icon. You should now see the projected sales figures for each data point of the chart corresponding to the months. Select the *Legend* icon and choose *None* to remove the series name from the chart; this is not necessary when you have only one variable that you are tracking as in this example. Since there is a slide title, you can also remove the chart title by selecting *Chart Title* and choosing *None*. The completed chart is shown in Figure 6.14.

FIGURE 6.14 Completed chart example

You can alter the font size for any of the text elements of the chart using the *Home* ribbon. You can also change the size of the chart manually by dragging the grip points on the corners and midpoints just as you can for any other object in PowerPoint. When you use a chart, it should take up the majority of the slide or it will likely not be readable to the audience. If you have specific points you want to make about the chart, you can add drawing objects to highlight particular data points rather than adding any text comments.

6.2.2 Chart Types

Charts can take a wide variety of forms, and different chart types are useful for representing different types of information. The common types of charts you will encounter (and can add to your presentations) include column, line, pie, area, and scatter charts; all of these types are constructed from underlying data of some form, although not all data can support all chart types. When choosing a chart type, you need to consider what information you want to present and how you want to present it. There are other forms of charts available for you to construct from your data, but those typically require an area of expertise beyond general use. The following sections provide a further explanation of some common chart types, along with examples of their usage so you can determine which charts are best for your own use.

6.2.3 Column Charts

A column chart is primarily used for comparisons, such as changes over time or a comparison of regions or countries. The best use of a column chart is when the highest column represents the optimal condition. When there are multiple columns coupled together, it is typically to show a comparison of parts of the same overall whole. Figure 6.15 shows an example of a column chart and the accompanying data to reproduce it.

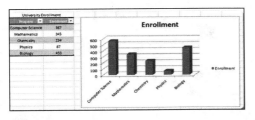

FIGURE 6.15 Column chart example

6.2.4 Line Charts

A line chart is used to track data over set intervals. In most cases, the data in each series has an existing (primarily linear) relationship and the points of data are connected. A line chart is a basic graphing tool that can be used to demonstrate a variety of data in a variety of circumstances; multiple series represent independent sets of observations that may or may not be interrelated. An example of a line chart is shown in Figure 6.16.

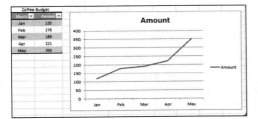

FIGURE 6.16 Line chart example

6.2.5 Pie Charts

A pie chart is a representation of the elements that comprise a total value. The visual display is a circle comparing the relative values of the components, typically as a percentage of the whole. A pie chart is best used when you want to showcase the proportional contribution of one element of the whole, such as the number of answers selected in a multiple-choice question. Pie charts are best used to illustrate a single item. An example of a pie chart is shown in Figure 6.17.

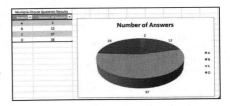

FIGURE 6.17 Pie chart example

6.2.6 Bar

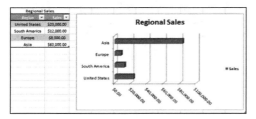

FIGURE 6.18 Bar chart example

A bar graph shows comparisons among individual items for a single observation. The stacked version of the bar graph compares elements that comprise a whole within each individual item. A representation of sales by region for a single quarter would be appropriate for a bar graph. Figure 6.18 shows an example bar graph and the data used to construct it.

6.2.7 Area

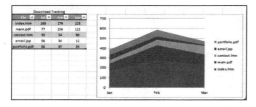

FIGURE 6.19 Area chart example

An area chart demonstrates how pieces contribute to a total value through multiple observations. Each piece in each observation should represent a piece of a total value. The area chart should demonstrate relative contributions and trends over time along with the overall trend of the total data measured. You can see an example of an area chart in Figure 6.19.

6.2.8 Scatter

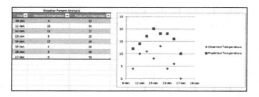

FIGURE 6.20 Scatter chart example

A scatter chart is best used to show data clustering or alignment between multiple series of data; it consists of points plotted on multiple axes without connections (or with nonlinear connections) between either the series or the consecutive points in the series. It assumes there is no defined relationship between points in the data series or at least significant enough variation that a linear connection would be inaccurate. An example of this type of chart would be a map of predictions versus observations in an area where the relationship is not linear, such as observed temperatures. An example of a scatter chart is shown in Figure 6.20.

ACTIVITY 6.3—CHART MODIFICATION

Create a new presentation and save it as *Activity6_3*. Add one of the chart types presented in this chapter using similar data to the example given. Use the context-sensitive chart tools to add all possible chart elements to the display of your chart. Change the display style of your chart using the available formatting tools. What options are provided for altering the appearance of your chart? When would this be beneficial in business and how does it help you convey information? Be sure to save your work.

6.3 ANIMATIONS

Animations are one way to call attention to a particular object or group in PowerPoint. These can be triggered either by advancing the slide or through timing to play automatically. Animations can help you emphasize a point or call out a particular visual element, but they can also be easily overused. The animations that you add to your presentation should be short and relevant. All of the settings for animations are housed in the *Animations* ribbon, shown in Figure 6.21.

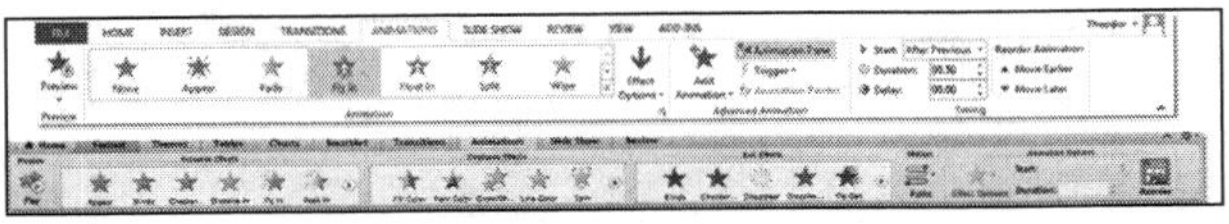

FIGURE 6.21 Animations ribbons in PowerPoint

To illustrate the concepts and mechanics of animation, you will add animation to the product demonstration slide in the *MySalesPitchNotes* project. The general categories of animation effects are Entrance, Emphasis, Exit, and Motion. Entrance effects are used to start an object (or group) off of the visible slide and transition it into its placement location; the animation will end with the element in the location where it was initially placed before any animation effects. Emphasis animations start and end with the object in the same location in which it started; this is used to highlight an object for attention. Exit animations are used to remove objects from the slide; these will begin with the object in its original place and end with the object no longer visible on the slide. Motion effects move an object from one position to another; the path for this motion and the beginning and end points can be changed.

To emphasize the hot dog character in the example, apply an emphasis effect like *Teeter* to it. To fly in the second step of creating the product, set the text box to *Fly In*. The arrow should simply fade into existence once the text box is in place, so a Fade effect is appropriate. You can customize any effects using the *Effect Options* icon; this will change to give you the options available for the current animation you have applied. It is possible to apply multiple animation effects to a single object as long as they do not conflict in motion (so you can use an emphasis effect with an entrance effect but not an entrance effect with an exit effect). You can preview your animation sequence from the *Animations* ribbon by clicking the *Preview* icon in PowerPoint 2013 and the *Play* icon in PowerPoint 2011. A completed example in *Normal* view is shown in Figure 6.22. This demonstrates the numbering shown for each sequence to let you know in which order the effects will play; numbers that are the same are part of the same sequence.

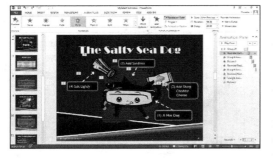

FIGURE 6.22 Complex animation sequence in Normal view in PowerPoint 2013

After you have added your animations, you can adjust their start condition, triggers, sequencing, and timing. If you added the animation effects in the order you want them to display, you do not need to rearrange them. However, if you want to change the order, open the *Animation* pane by clicking its icon from the *Animations* ribbon in PowerPoint 2013; to open the equivalent *Custom Animation* pane in PowerPoint 2011, click the *Reorder* icon in the *Animations* ribbon. With the *Animation* pane open, use the *Move Earlier* and *Move Later* icons on the *Animations* ribbon in PowerPoint 2013 (or the up and down arrows at the bottom of the *Animation* pane in either PowerPoint 2013 or PowerPoint 2011) to reorder your animation sequence. You can also click and drag an item within the *Animation* pane to change its position within the animation order.

The *Start* condition is the action that starts the animation sequence. By default, this is set to *On Click*, which is the same as a slide advance operationally. If you do not want to have to click for each animation to begin, you can change the trigger to *With Previous* or *After Previous*. Setting the animation to *With Previous* starts the selected animation as soon as the previous animation begins; setting the animation to *After Previous* will start the animation sequence after the previous animation sequence has completed. You can change this setting in the *Animations* ribbon or the *Animation* pane for the currently selected animation.

NOTE *When you are sharing your presentation for viewing on a personal computer, you should avoid using the On Click start condition for animation. It is annoying to a viewer to have to repeatedly click just to get access to the information a slide has to offer. The On Click start condition may assist you in presenting, but you should change it to* After Previous *before you share your slides for individual use later.*

The *Timing* panel contains the duration and delay settings for each animation sequence. The *Timing* panel is part of the *Animations* ribbon in PowerPoint 2013 but is located on the *Custom Animation* pane in PowerPoint 2011. The duration is how long the animation sequence takes to complete; most animations should occur quickly so they do not waste any significant time in the presentation (the preset selections for timing have a minimum of 0.5 seconds and a maximum of 5 seconds). The delay is how long the sequence will pause before starting when the start condition is reached; you should use delays sparingly and only when necessary for presenting the content.

If you do not want your animation to play as part of the normal slide progression in PowerPoint 2013, you can change the Trigger *attribute. The trigger attribute is what causes the animation to start; by default it is set to take input from the presentation timing and standard presentation advances. However, you can change the trigger to a click of any object within the current slide; this will function like an action setting to start the animation sequence.*

You can optionally add sounds to your animation sequences from the *Animation* pane (or *Custom Animation* pane) using the *Effect Options* selection. You can access *Effect Options* from the drop-down menu for the sequence entry in PowerPoint 2013; this is a foldout panel for the animation sequence in PowerPoint 2011. You can also set how you want your text animated, either by word or by letter, and the delay between text sequences in the animation. The text settings can be changed using *Effect Options* in PowerPoint 2013 and the separate foldout *Text Animations* panel in PowerPoint 2011.

ACTIVITY 6.4—ANIMATION

Create a new presentation and save it as *Activity6_4*. Add a slide to the presentation and add two different clip art elements to the slide. Add different animation effects to each clip art element and preview them in Slide Show View. Use the Animation Pane to reorder the animation and repeat the preview. Now, change one of the animations for a clip art element and repeat the preview. How can these tools be used to create more complex animations in a slide? When should this level of animation be used? Be sure to save your work.

CHAPTER SUMMARY

This chapter covered the more advanced media elements that you can include in your slide show presentations. You must always keep your audience and the method of delivery in mind when creating your slides so that they deliver the maximum impact to your audience instead of just providing information. The next chapter of the text covers the advanced features of presentation software, including how to construct handouts for your slides to assist in your presentation and even how to export your slides as images to use in other documents and applications.

CHAPTER KNOWLEDGE CHECK

1. Once you have added animation effects to a slide, you cannot change the order in which they occur.
   a. True
   b. False

2. The following type of media requires support from a spreadsheet to calculate the display:
    a. Table
    b. Chart
    c. Animation
    d. All of the above
    e. None of the above

3. In general, audio and video increase the file size of a presentation more drastically than other media elements.
    a. True
    b. False

4. Tables are a good form of media to use when presenting a large volume of information (at least 10 rows by 6 columns) because they are clear to the audience at the back of the room.
    a. True
    b. False

5. SmartArt is a tool that allows for quick creation of professional-looking graphics, but SmartArt graphics can be adequately created using drawing objects and text boxes.
    a. True
    b. False

PRACTICE EXERCISES

- Research a topic in computing and create a 10-slide presentation explaining the topic. Include at least three of the media types in your presentation to assist in your explanation.
- For this exercise you will use the PowerPoint presentation you developed in the Chapter 5. You will open the presentation and begin editing it according to the following instructions: make your logo include at least two animations, add some type of background music to your presentation, include a graphic using SmartArt, and include an applicable video clip that you either found on the Internet or developed yourself.
- Create two different charts in a PowerPoint presentation. Be sure they contain different data and they are appropriate for the type of data being displayed. Compare the two charts to determine which one is easier to explain to an audience and what information each one conveys that the data itself would not readily show.
- Create and save a new PowerPoint presentation. Using either your own video or Clip Art from Office.com, add and modify a video in a slide. Test the video within your presentation by viewing it in Slide Show View. Next, format the video with effects. View the presentation in Slide Show View

and activate the video again. How does the display change when you apply the formatting? In what circumstance would you want the effects added to a video to enhance its presentation to the audience? Is there a risk of distracting the audience from the video content with this approach? Explain your answer with examples.

CHAPTER 7

ADVANCED FEATURES OF PRESENTATION SOFTWARE

This chapter focuses on some of the more advanced techniques for enhancing and supplementing your presentations. You will learn how to create handouts to accompany your slide decks and how to optimize your slides and reshape the basic slide layout. You will also learn how to edit presentations and even export your slides as individual images for use elsewhere. When you have completed the chapter, you will be able to:

- Format and create handout pages to accompany your presentation
- Configure slide properties and define custom sizes and layouts
- Export your slides as image files

7.1 CREATING HANDOUTS

When you create a presentation, particularly one that is being presented live, you may want to also create handouts that you can distribute to your audience. You should make sure that any handouts you provide continue the narrative of the presentation in a way that enhances the audience's understanding. You should also be careful not to give out your handouts too soon, especially not before you present or as you begin your presentation. Your audience is always going to be more apt to pay attention to what is in their hands than what they are being shown or told.

There are two main types of handouts commonly distributed with a presentation; these are either miniature versions of the slides themselves as handout pages or a combination of the slide and the accompanying notes in notes pages. You can also print the slides themselves at one slide per page or print just an outline of your presentation, which contains only the text elements of your slides without the

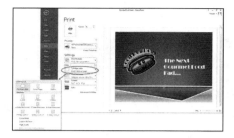

FIGURE 7.1 Print options for PowerPoint 2013

theme and background design or formatting and effects. You can preview this outline at any time by selecting the *Outline* tab in the *Slides/Outline* pane. The options for printing any of the handout types are available from the *Print* icon under the *File* menu in PowerPoint 2013, as shown in Figure 7.1. In PowerPoint 2011, you select the type of handout you want to print in the *Print What* entry of the standard Print dialog box (accessed by selecting *Print* from the *File* menu).

7.1.1 Modifying the Handout Master

FIGURE 7.2 Handout Master interface in PowerPoint 2013

The Handout Master will be used as a template automatically in PowerPoint whenever you are printing multiple slides per page. In PowerPoint 2013, you can customize the Handout Master by selecting the *View* ribbon and selecting *Handout Master*. This will open a context-sensitive *Handout Master* ribbon, shown in Figure 7.2. The *Design* ribbon will once again disappear until you close the Handout Master by clicking the *Close Master View* icon. To access the Handout Master in PowerPoint 2011, select the *Themes* ribbon, choose *Edit Master*, and then select *Handout Master*.

The options in the *Handout Master* ribbon allow you to make any of the four text boxes in the header and footer of the document visible or invisible. You can edit the contents of these text boxes in the preview document where you ordinarily see the slide you are creating. The default number of slides per page can be set in this ribbon, but you can alter that setting when you print the document. You will not see a preview of your slides on this page, and you cannot edit the slide contents while the Handout Master is open.

The text boxes in this master can accept text effects just like text boxes in any other slide. This means you can change the font, add effects, and change the font color and size. It is usually a good idea to at least change the font to match the rest of the presentation. When you are creating handouts, you are changing your presentation from a primarily visual medium to a printed one, so you need to keep the consistency of the entire package in mind. The font and color selections for the Handout Master affect this page only (and the printed pages that are based on it) and will not alter the design of the slides themselves.

7.1.2 Modifying the Notes Master

If you followed along with the example project in Chapters 5 and 6, you should have substantial outline notes in your sales pitch presentation. If that is the case, you can simply open your *MySalesPitch* file and work from it. If you want to use an existing example to see how the Notes function works, you can open the *MySalesPitchNotes* presentation from the companion resources.

With your presentation open in PowerPoint 2013, click on the *View* ribbon and select *Notes Master*. This will open the Notes Master view, which has its own context-sensitive *Notes Master* ribbon, as shown in Figure 7.3. To access the Notes Master in PowerPoint 2011, select the *Themes* ribbon, choose *Edit Master*, and then select *Notes Master*.

You can format any of the header and footer placeholders in this view using text effects and the font and paragraph settings. You also have the option of setting a background style for the pages, but remember that the text elements need to be legible in print and any background you add will increase ink consumption. Be sure to also consider the quality of the handouts you will be printing when choosing to alter the color scheme of the text; if you are printing in grayscale, using a lot of color in the text boxes or for the background is not a good idea.

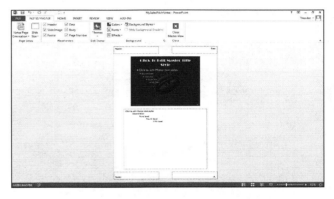

FIGURE 7.3 Notes Master interface in PowerPoint 2013

> **NOTE**
>
> *While background options are not included in the main ribbon interface, you can format the background in PowerPoint 2011 by using the right-click menu. Just right-click inside of the page and select* Format Background; *this will allow you to alter the background as you would any other object.*

The notes that have been written in the slides themselves will be formatted using the options you set in the placeholder text box for the notes in this view; this is where you can add effects such as shadows and reflections to your notes. However, you should make sure the effects fit with the theme of the presentation and the notes are readable in print format. You do not have the restrictions of screen projection to consider with the notes formatting, but the notes should be treated the same as any printed document. The outline levels in the notes text box of the Notes Master view can be formatted the same way as the outline levels of the Slide Master in the Slide Master view. You can alter the position of any of the text boxes on this screen as well, but the default layout is optimal for printing. Double-clicking the preview of the slide will open the Slide Master view and allow you to edit the Slide Master.

ACTIVITY 7.1—THE NOTES MASTER

Using the presentation for this chapter, modify the Notes Master to change the display of the slides in this view. Do these changes carry over to the normal view of the slides? When would you want to make changes to the slide display in this view instead of the Normal View? What options are available for formatting the text within the slide compared to the text of the notes themselves? Explore these options and save your presentation as *Activity7_1*.

7.2 EDITING PRESENTATIONS

You may not always be working on a presentation document that you create yourself. You also may not be able to create the entire project at once, so it is important to be able to open and edit existing presentation documents. You can change most of the properties of a PowerPoint presentation while it is open, regardless of when it was created or by whom.

If you download a presentation or open it from an email message, PowerPoint will restrict the editing options of the document, allowing you to read it without running any additional scripts attached to the document (called macros) and without activating any of the ribbons to alter the content. Once you click the *Enable Editing* button on the warning that appears, you will be able to manipulate and edit the document as usual.

7.2.1 Opening and Editing Existing Presentations

You can open presentations from the *File* menu by selecting the *Open* option; use this to open the *MyBrokenRobot* file from the companion resources for this text. This file has only one slide with a robot whose arms have fallen off of its body. It is your task to reposition and reattach them. Notice that when you open a presentation document, any presentation documents that are already open will remain open in separate windows.

Use your mouse cursor to select each arm and position it on the slide where it can reasonably connect to the shoulder socket of the robot; do not overlap the shapes because you are going to use connector lines to attach the arms. Now use the rotation option to rotate the arm back into position. Add a drawing object connector line from the arm to the shoulder socket.

NOTE *Any animation applied to objects that are connected by a connecting line will not animate the connecting line itself. Instead, the line will remain in the initial fixed position for both objects, ignoring any animation movements unless they are part of a group to which animation is applied. If both objects are not part of the same group, the connecting line will ignore the object that is not part of the group in terms of positioning and movement.*

Repeat the steps for the other arm. Change the robot's frown to a smile using the yellow diamond controller for the mouth setting. Finally, change the title of the presentation: Use the strikethrough formatting on the word

"Broken" and add the word *Fixed* beside it. Remember to send the connector lines you added to the back of the slide layering so they do not appear above the animation of the robot. A completed example is shown in Figure 7.4.

You can also change the theme and the colors of this presentation to better suit your preferences. The colors will automatically adapt when you change the theme in PowerPoint,

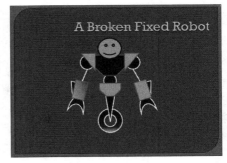

FIGURE 7.4 Completed example

but you can change your color preference after selecting the theme. Save the completed project as *MyFixedRobot*.

ACTIVITY 7.2—ANIMATION

Using the *MyBrokenRobot* presentation, use animation to repair the robot following the steps outlined in this section. Keep in mind the different actions that you can take with animation and the different changes and effects that can be applied. Play your animation to test the results, which should show the robot being repaired. How does the resulting slide appear in the normal view for designing your slides? Save your presentation as *Activity7_2*.

7.2.2 Slide Setup and Slide Orientation

You can set the size of your slides and the slide orientation. If you are presenting your slides on a normal screen or standard projector, you do not need to change the slide size from the default. The default aspect ratio is the best option for standard use. (Although PowerPoint can be used to create brochures and other publications, this is not its primary use.) For this example, select a slide size that is equivalent to standard paper printouts. To change the slide size, click the *Slide Size* icon on the *Design* ribbon in PowerPoint 2013. This will open the *Page Setup* dialog box shown in Figure 7.5. In PowerPoint 2011, you can change the slide size by selecting *Slide Size* from the *Themes* ribbon or by selecting the *File* menu and choosing *Page Setup*.

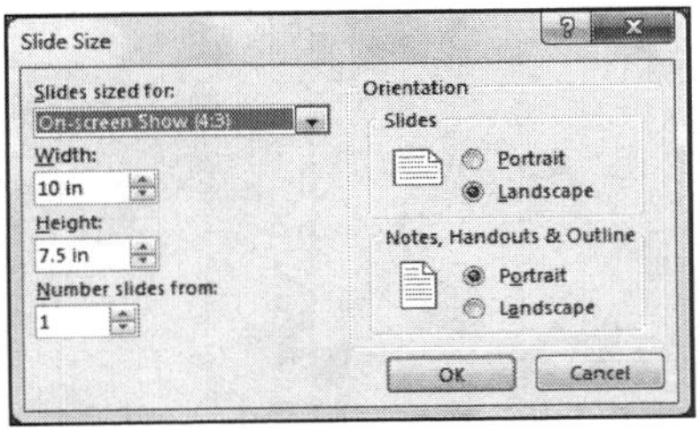

In this dialog box, you can set your slide size to any of the predefined standard sizes or a custom size. It is possible to use PowerPoint to create a poster image (such as those needed for professional research conference presentations), but the maximum size setting of a slide for either the height or the width is 56 inches. That means the largest poster you can create is 56" by 56". If your planned project

FIGURE 7.5 Slide Size dialog box in PowerPoint 2013

fits within that size limitation, your only concern is how to get it printed. Once you export your poster image from PowerPoint to a Portable Document Format (PDF) file, most professional print shops will accept that format.

> **NOTE** *Changing the aspect ratio with content in your slide will change the aspect ratio of the content as well, which may distort images and drawing objects already in your presentation. Therefore, you should try to set the slide size before you start creating the content for your presentation.*

The *Slide Size* dialog box also allows you to set your slide orientation; that is, whether you want it to display in landscape layout (the default where the width is greater than the height) or portrait layout (the standard layout for text documents and printing). You can change this setting for the slides and any printed handout separately. In PowerPoint 2013, you can set the starting number of the slides in this dialog box; it defaults to starting at one for the first slide of the presentation.

7.2.3 Creating a Custom Layout

If you find that you need slides with a particular arrangement of elements that is not provided in any of the default layouts, you can create a custom layout in PowerPoint. To do this, open the *Slide Master* view and find the *Insert Layout* icon (or *New Layout* icon in PowerPoint 2011) on the *Slide Master* ribbon. Clicking this icon creates a new child layout slide from the main Slide Master. This new slide will initially contain only a title and footer placeholders. You can add additional placeholders to the new layout slide by clicking the *Insert Placeholder* icon to open the menu that allows you to choose the content type for the placeholder. The default Content placeholder includes quick links to all of the available media elements, while the other options allow specific media and text. The Insert Placeholder drop-down menu is shown in Figure 7.6.

When you have finished creating your new layout, click the *Rename* icon to name your new layout for use in the presentation. When you save the presentation and close the *Slide Master* view, the new layout you created will be available as a selection in the *Layout* icon menu of the *Home* ribbon.

The name that displays for the layout will reflect what you renamed it; if you did not perform this step, the name will default to "Custom Layout." This custom layout will exist only in the presentation in which you created it; it will not be available for use in other presentation documents.

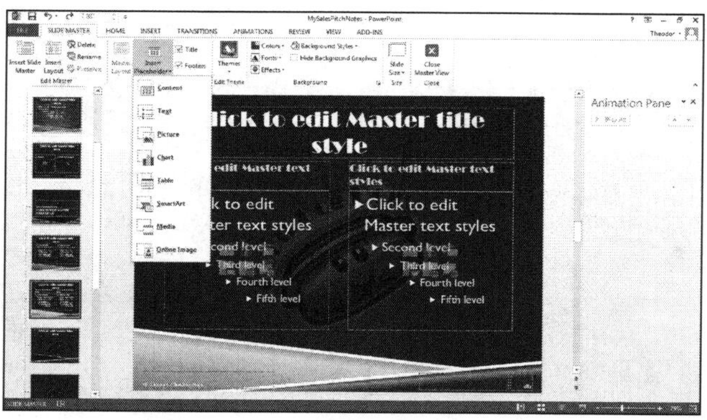

FIGURE 7.6 Custom layout creation and Insert Placeholder menu in PowerPoint 2013

7.2.4 Hiding and Showing Slides

If you need to shorten your presentation to fit a specific time slot or you need to slightly tailor the same presentation for different audiences, you may have some slides that you do not need but that you do not want to delete. For instance, you may have a slide with background information that is not necessary for the general audience, but you may need it if someone asks a particular question. To keep a slide in your presentation without including it in the normal *Slide Show* view, you can utilize the option to hide the slide.

To hide a slide, select the slide you want hidden and open the *Slide Show* ribbon. Click the *Hide Slide* icon. This will gray out the slide in the *Slides/ Outline* pane to indicate it is hidden. You can still continue to edit the slide, but it will not display during your presentation.

NOTE *The* Hide Slide *icon is a toggle. When it is highlighted, the slide is hidden. When you click the icon again, the slide will be visible in the presentation. A hidden slide retains its slide number, so if you have slide numbers visible, the presentation will skip the number of the hidden slide.*

If you need to access a hidden slide during your presentation, select the slide manually by right-clicking within the presentation while *Slide Show* view is active, choosing *Go to Slide*, and then selecting the slide number and title you want to display. You can also create an action object to point directly to the hidden slide; if you need to view the slide during the presentation, click the action object and the slide will display.

ACTIVITY 7.3—ACTIONS AND HIDDEN SLIDES

Using the active presentation for the project for this chapter, select one of the objects within the SmartArt graphic to link to the previous (and now hidden) contact slide. Add an action to the object, choose *Slide* as the *Link to* value, and select the hidden slide. Save your presentation as *Activity 7_3* and test your presentation to make sure it works.

7.3 OPTIMIZING AND EXPORTING IMAGES FROM SLIDES

Adding a large amount of media to your presentation may cause some issues with the file size of the document. If you are emailing the document or presenting it on another machine, you have to consider how easy it is to transfer it from one location to another. Depending on how you are using the document, you can perform some tasks to compress the file size of your presentation while retaining all of the media you have added. If the presentation document is just for use on a computer screen, compressing the images will reduce the file size without sacrificing the media quality. If you are printing your slides on a high-quality printer, compressing them may not be the best choice.

7.3.1 Compressing Images

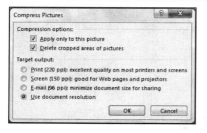

FIGURE 7.7 Compress Pictures dialog box in PowerPoint 2013

To compress your images, select an image in your presentation and open the *Format* ribbon for Picture Tools. Select the *Compress Pictures* icon (or *Compress* in PowerPoint 2011). This will open the *Compress Pictures* dialog box shown in Figure 7.7. From here, you can select the resolution you want for your image. You can also set whether you want the cropped areas of the image removed and whether you want to apply these settings to all of the images in the document or just the one you have selected (deselecting the *Apply only to this picture* checkbox in PowerPoint 2013 will apply the setting to all images in the presentation document).

7.3.2 Exporting Slides as Images

Your presentation slides can be exported as images from PowerPoint. To do this, simply open the *File* menu and choose *Save As*. The common formats for images are GIF Graphics Interchange Format, JPEG File Interchange Format, TIFF Tag Image File Format, PNG Portable Network Graphics Format, and Device Independent Bitmap. Select the format in which you wish to save your slides; you will be asked whether you want to save the current slide only or every slide in the chosen format. With PowerPoint 2011, it is better to use the *Save as Pictures* command from the *File* menu; this allows you to open an *Options* dialog box in which you can specify more detailed image options for the format.

7.3.3 Common Image Formats

There are a number of different file formats for image content. Typical image file formats are JPEG (Joint Photographic Experts Group) File Interchange Format, Graphics Interchange Format (GIF), Bitmap, Portable Network Graphic (PNG), and Tag Image File Format (TIFF). All of these have specific characteristics and uses, but they are not all suited to the every application. The primary distinction between these formats is how the visual

A *lossless* format describes a file format that does not lose pixel or color information from the original image source. These tend to be larger files than compresses, lossy formats.

A *lossy* format describes a file format that loses pixel or color information from the original image source. These tend to be compressed and have a smaller file size than lossless formats.

A *palette* is the range of colors that an image file format can contain. Some formats have a limited palette, such as GIF. Most lossless formats allow a truecolor palette, which contains 16 million colors.

information is stored in the file and how much of the information is retained from the original source. This is known as *lossless* and *lossy* formats.

The file formats you should become familiar with for images are the following:

- **Bitmap and TIFF**: These are lossless image formats. They tend to have larger file sizes but they retain all of the image information. Their support for display on the Web is mostly legacy and these are not recommended as the final format for your images. However, these are great formats to use on a working copy of an image that you are going to convert to a JPG or PNG.
- **GIF**: A GIF image is a limited-palette image that can support 256 colors per image. It is good for images with large areas of the same color but performs poorly for images with gradients and dithering. The GIF format allows image transparency and it has an animated version which rotates through a sequence of GIF images using the same color palette. Because of its limitations and the restrictions on creating files in this format, it has largely disappeared from modern Websites. You should only use this format if you have a specific need for lightweight animation; otherwise you should use the PNG format for transparency.
- **PNG**: The PNG format was created as an open-source successor to the GIF format. The PNG format supports a *truecolor* (16 million colors) palette and allows image transparency. This is an excellent format for layering images and it is fully supported in modern browsers.
- **JPEG**: The JPEG (or JPG) format is a lossy, compressed format that is well-suited to photographs and complex images. This is a well-supported and highly recommended format for images on the Web. The compression method of JPEG files does not work well for images with a large section of the same color; in this case, PNG is the better format to use even though the file size is larger.

ACTIVITY 7.4—IMAGE EXPORTS

Using the presentation for this chapter, practice exporting the slides as images. What options are you given when you save the slides as an image format? How are the files saved on your machine? Try opening the saved files. What program opens them by default on your machine?

CHAPTER SUMMARY

This chapter covered the more advanced topics for editing presentations, changing the slide size, and adding handouts to your presentation. Presentation software can also allow you to create customized images at different sizes through the export feature, which is a useful tool if you need to create graphics quickly and do not have an advanced graphics editing program available.

You should now have the necessary skills to create dynamic and media rich presentations!

CHAPTER KNOWLEDGE CHECK

1. Hidden slides are not assigned a number in the slide show. When they are shown again, they change the numbering of the slides that follow them in the presentation.
   a. True
   b. False

2. The following is an image format that is common for exporting presentation slides:
   a. GIF
   b. TIFF
   c. JPEG
   d. All of the above
   e. None of the above

3. Slides can be formatted differently for handouts and for presentation within the same file.
   a. True
   b. False

4. You can design your own layout slide that includes placeholders for different types of content in PowerPoint.
   a. True
   b. False

5. Notes that you add to a slide are visible to the audience during Slide Show View.
   a. True
   b. False

PRACTICE EXERCISES

1. Return back to the grand opening PowerPoint presentation you modified. You will now need to go back and develop an appropriate outline. Use this outline to create handouts and notes to have at the grand opening. This will give your audience something tangible to walk away with, helping you and your company to stay fresh in their mind.

2. Using the *MyFixedRobot* project you created in this chapter, change the slide size to a poster size of 24" by 36" and add captions and a logo to the slide so it looks like an advertisement poster. Save your document as

HugeFixedRobot and export it as an image file using both the GIF and JPEG formats. In a separate word processing document of at least 200 words, compare the two images that were produced in terms of image quality, text quality, color, and file size.

3. Create notes for each slide in the presentation which you have modified throughout this chapter. Be sure they are detailed and describe the contents of the slide and what you want to say about each slide. How can these be used to help you prepare to present your presentation live in front of an audience? When would these be suitable for handouts? Explore the formatting options for handouts and describe the strategy for complementing your presentation with the text you add in this format.

4. Create a presentation with six slides and practice adding content to each slide. Hide the even numbered slides and create an Action on each odd slide to show the hidden even slide immediately after it. Start the presentation from the beginning in Slide Show View. Run the show once without clicking any of the Action items you added. Next, run it again and click each action item as you encounter the slides. How does the presentation behave differently in each run (with and without using the Actions)? When would this be beneficial to apply in a presentation? Explain your answer with examples.

INDEX